W9-ADP-872

WITHDRAWN

Gramley Library
Salem College
Winston-Salem, NC 27108

CHARLOTTE HAWKINS BROWN

"MAMMY"

An Appeal to the Heart of the South

THE CORRECT THING TO DO—
TO SAY—TO WEAR

AFRICAN-AMERICAN WOMEN WRITERS, 1910–1940

HENRY LOUIS GATES, JR. *General Editor*

Jennifer Burton *Associate Editor*

OTHER VOLUMES IN THIS SERIES

CHARLOTTE HAWKINS BROWN

"MAMMY"
An Appeal to the Heart of the South

THE CORRECT THING TO DO—TO SAY— TO WEAR

Introduction by
CAROLYN C. DENARD

G.K. HALL & CO.
An Imprint of Simon & Schuster Macmillan
New York

Prentice Hall International
London   Mexico City   New Delhi   Singapore   Sydney   Toronto

Gramley Library
Salem College
Winston-Salem, NC 27108

Introduction copyright © 1995 by Carolyn C. Denard

All rights reserved. No part of this book may be reproduced or transmitted in any form or by any means, electronic or mechanical, including photocopying, recording, or by any information storage and retrieval system, without permission in writing from the Publisher.

G.K. Hall & Co.
An Imprint of Simon & Schuster Macmillan
866 Third Avenue
New York, NY 10022

Library of Congress Catalog Card Number: 94-42137

Printed in the United States of America

Printing Number
1 2 3 4 5 6 7 8 9 10

Library of Congress Cataloging-in-Publication Data
The Library of Congress has catalogued the hardcover edition of this book as follows:

Brown, Charlotte Hawkins, 1883–1961.
[Mammy]
Mammy : an appeal to the heart of the South ; and, The correct thing to do—to say—to wear / Charlotte Hawkins Brown ; introduction by Carolyn C. Denard.
p. cm. — (African American women writers, 1910–1940)
First work originally published: 1919. 2nd work originally published: 1941.
Includes bibliographical references.
ISBN 0-8161-1632-6 (alk. paper)
1. Afro-American women—Southern States—Fiction. 2. Women domestics—Southern States—Fiction. 3. Clothing and dress. 4. Etiquette. I. Title. II. Title: Correct thing to do—to say—to wear. III. Series.
PS3503.R793M3   1995
813'.52—dc20   94-42137
                                                                              CIP
ISBN (hardcover) 0-8161-1632-6
ISBN (paperback) 0-7838-1395-3

This paper meets the requirements of ANSI/NISO Z39.48-1992 (Permanence of Paper).

CONTENTS

GENERAL EDITORS' PREFACE

The past decade of our literary history might be thought of as the era of African-American women writers. Culminating in the awarding of the Pulitzer Prize to Toni Morrison and Rita Dove and the Nobel Prize for Literature to Toni Morrison in 1993, and characterized by the presence of several writers—Toni Morrison, Alice Walker, Maya Angelou, and the Delany Sisters, among others—on the *New York Times* Best Seller List, the shape of the most recent period in our literary history has been determined in large part by the writings of black women.

This, of course, has not always been the case. African-American women authors have been publishing their thoughts and feelings at least since 1773, when Phillis Wheatley published her book of poems in London, thereby bringing poetry directly to bear upon the philosophical discourse over the African's "place in nature" and his or her place in the great chain of being. The scores of words published by black women in America in the nineteenth century—most of which were published in extremely limited editions and never reprinted—have been republished in new critical editions in the forty-volume *Schomburg Library of Nineteenth-Century Black Women Writers*. The critical response to that series has led to requests from scholars and students alike for a similar series, one geared to the work by black women published between 1910 and the beginning of World War Two.

African-American Women Writers, 1910–1940 is designed to bring back into print many writers who otherwise would be unknown to contemporary readers, and to increase the availability of lesser-known texts by established writers who originally published during this critical period in African-American letters. This series implicitly acts as a chronological sequel to the Schomburg series, which focused on the origins of the black female literary tradition in America.

In less than a decade, the study of African-American women's writings has grown from its promising beginnings into a firmly established field in departments of English, American Studies, and African-American Studies. A comparison of the form and function of the original series and this sequel illustrates this dramatic shift. The *Schomburg Library* was published at the cusp of focused academic investigation into the interplay between race and gender. It covered the extensive period from the publication of Phillis Wheatley's *Poems on Various Subjects, Religious and Moral* in 1773 through the "Black Women's Era" of 1890–1910, and was designed to be an inclusive series of the major early texts by black women writers. The Schomburg Library provided a historical backdrop for black women's writings of the 1970s and 1980s, including the works of writers such as Toni Morrison, Alice Walker, Maya Angelou, and Rita Dove.

African-American Women Writers, 1910–1940 continues our effort to provide a new generation of readers access to texts—historical, sociological, and literary—that have been largely "unread" for most of this century. The series bypasses works that are important both to the period and the tradition, but that are readily available, such as Zora Neale Hurston's *Their Eyes Were Watching God*, Jessie Fauset's *Plum Bun* and *There is Confusion*, and Nella Larsen's *Quicksand* and *Passing*. Our goal is to provide access to a wide variety of rare texts. The series includes Fauset's two other novels, *The Chinaberry Tree: A Novel of American Life* and *Comedy: American Style*, and Hurston's short play, *Color Struck*, since these are not yet widely available. It also features works by virtually unknown writers, such as *A Tiny Spark*, Christina Moody's slim volume of poetry self-published in 1910, and *Reminiscences of School Life, and Hints on Teaching*, written by Fanny Jackson Coppin in the last year of her life (1913), a multi-genre work combining an autobiographical sketch and reflections on trips to England and South Africa, complete with pedagogical advice.

Cultural studies' investment in diverse resources allows the historic scope of the *African-American Women Writers* series to be more focused than the *Schomburg Library* series, which covered works written over a 137-year period. With few exceptions, the authors included in the *African-American Women Writers* series wrote their major works between 1910 and 1940. The texts reprinted include all of the works by each particular author that are not otherwise readily obtainable. As a result, two volumes contain works originally published after 1940. The Charlotte Hawkins Brown volume includes her book of etiquette published in 1941, *The Correct Thing To Do—To Say—To Wear*. One of the poetry volumes contains Maggie Pogue Johnson's *Fallen Blossoms*, published in 1951, a compilation of all her previously published and unpublished poems.

Excavational work by scholars during the past decade has been crucial to the development of *African-American Women Writers, 1910–1940*. Germinal bibliographic sources such as Anne Allen Shockley's *Afro-American Women Writers 1746–1933* and Maryemma Graham's *Database of African-American Women Writers* made the initial identification of texts possible. Other works were brought to our attention by scholars who wrote letters sharing their research. Additional texts by selected authors were then added, so that many volumes contain the complete oeuvres of particular writers. Pieces by authors without enough published work to fill an entire volume were grouped with other pieces by genre.

The two types of collections, those organized by author and those organized by genre, bring out different characteristics of black women's writings of the period. The collected works of the literary writers illustrate that many of them were experimenting with a variety of forms. Mercedes Gilbert's volume, for example, contains her 1931 collection, *Selected Gems of Poetry, Comedy, and Drama, Etc.*, as well as her 1938 novel, *Aunt Sara's Wooden God*. Georgia Douglas Johnson's volume contains her plays and short stories in addition to her poetry. Sarah Lee Brown Fleming's volume combines her 1918 novel *Hope's Highway* with her 1920 collection of poetry, *Clouds and Sunshine*.

The generic volumes both bring out the formal and thematic similarities among many of the writings and highlight the striking individuality of particular writers. Most of the plays in the volume of one-acts are social dramas whose tragic endings can be clearly attributed to miscegenation and racism. Within the context of these other plays, Marita Bonner's surrealistic theatrical vision becomes all the more striking.

The volumes of *African-American Women Writers, 1910–1940* contain reproductions of more than one hundred previously published texts, including twenty-nine plays, seventeen poetry collections, twelve novels, six autobiographies, five collections of short biographical sketches, three biographies, three histories of organizations, three black histories, two anthologies, two sociological studies, a diary, and a book of etiquette. Each volume features an introduction written by a contemporary scholar that provides crucial biographical data on each author and the historical and critical context of her work. In some cases, little information on the authors was available outside of the fragments of biographical data contained in the original introduction or in the text itself. In these instances, editors have documented the libraries and research centers where they tried to find information, in the hope that subsequent scholars will continue the necessary search to find the "lost" clues to the women's stories in the rich stores of papers, letters, photographs, and other primary materials scattered throughout the country that have yet to be fully catalogued.

Many of the thrilling moments that occurred during the development of this series were the result of previously fragmented pieces of these women's histories suddenly coming together, such as Adele Alexander's uncovering of an old family photograph, picturing her own aunt with Addie Hunton, the author Alexander was researching. Claudia Tate's examination of Georgia Douglas Johnson's papers in the Moorland-Spingarn Research Center of Howard University resulted in the discovery of a wealth of previously unpublished work.

The slippery quality of race itself emerged during the construction of the series. One of the short novels originally intended for inclusion in the series had to be cut when the family of the author protested that the writer was not of African descent. Another case involved Louise Kennedy's sociological study *The Negro Peasant Turns Inward*. The fact that none of the available biographical material on Kennedy specifically mentioned race, combined with some coded criticism in a review in the *Crisis*, convinced editor Sheila Smith McCoy that Kennedy was probably white.

These women, taken together, begin to chart the true vitality, and complexity, of the literary tradition that African-American women have generated, using a wide variety of forms. They testify to the fact that the monumental works of Hurston, Larsen, and Fauset, for example, emerged out of a larger cultural context; they were not exceptions or aberrations. Indeed, their contributions to American literature and culture, as this series makes clear, were fundamental not only to the shaping of the African-American tradition but to the American tradition as well.

Henry Louis Gates, Jr.
Jennifer Burton

PUBLISHER'S NOTE

In the *African-American Women Writers, 1910-1940* series, G.K. Hall not only is making available previously neglected works that, in many cases, have been long out of print; we are also, whenever possible, publishing these works in facsimiles reprinted from their original editions including, when available, reproductions of original title pages, copyright pages, and photographs.

When it was not possible for us to reproduce a complete facsimile edition of a particular work (for example, if the original exists only as a handwritten draft or is too fragile to be reproduced), we have attempted to preserve the essence of the original by resetting the work exactly as it originally appeared. Therefore, any typographical errors, strikeouts, or other anomalies reflect our efforts to give the reader a true sense of the original work.

We trust that these facsimile and reprint editions, together with the new introductory essays, will be both useful and historically enlightening to scholars and students alike.

INTRODUCTION

BY CAROLYN C. DENARD

In 1947, at the forty-fifth anniversary celebration of Palmer Memorial Institute, those present acknowledged the successful fund-raising on behalf of the Institute by its founder and president, Dr. Charlotte Hawkins Brown. Her efforts, now totalling more than one and one half million dollars, had been done with two aims in mind: "to produce refined graduates not ashamed to work but intent upon good performance in their respective academic and functional fields, and to establish good will and understanding between the races"[1] Indeed these two aims—"to produce refined graduates" and "to establish good will and understanding between the races"—describe not only the fundraising efforts of Charlotte Hawkins Brown but all of her life and work. As founder and builder of Palmer Memorial Institute, as organizer and president of the North Carolina State Federation of Negro Women's Clubs, as member of the Commission on Interracial Cooperation, and as noted lecturer, teacher, and community activist, Charlotte Hawkins Brown always worked on two fronts—within the black community, in order to improve the knowledge and opportunities of her own people; and outside the community, in order to change the hearts and minds of those who oppressed blacks.[2]

Her two published works, *Mammy: An Appeal to the Heart of the South* (1919) and *The Correct Thing To Do—To Say—To Wear* (1941), reprinted in this volume, are symbolic of the dual strategy Brown used in education and race work.[3] These two books—the first, an open appeal to white southerners in the form of a sentimental narrative describing their debt to blacks for past wrongs, and the other, a listing of the "social graces" that she believed young black men and women needed to know in order to supplement their formal education—represent profoundly the two-pronged strategy for racial uplift that characterized Brown's career.

As an educated African-American woman who grew up in the late-nineteenth and early-twentieth century, Charlotte Hawkins Brown was greatly affected by the goals of progress and reform to which she devoted her life. A contemporary of Mary McCleod Bethune, Booker T. Washington, Mary Church Terrell and others who stood at the vanguard of an important period of advancement and reform in African-American history, Brown was influenced by the spirit of racial uplift that characterized the era, and she was determined to make a difference in the lives of her people—only one generation removed from slavery. She knew the difficulties blacks faced and was willing to engage in a pioneering effort to help them work toward their own social, educational, and economic uplift. However, she also felt that there was a debt that whites owed to blacks for their loyal and unremunerated service during slavery. Generous philanthropy born from a fair sense of *noblesse oblige* on the part of whites, she believed, combined with earnest, individual efforts in academic education and social refinement on the part of blacks was the formula for breaking down the racial oppression which blacks suffered and for achieving harmony between the races.

That Brown believed in the possibility of the success of both these strategies for advancement was largely due to her own life experience. She was born 11 June 1883 in Henderson, North Carolina. Her grandparents had been slaves in Vance County, North Carolina. Her grandmother, Rebecca, was a house servant whose father was the master of the plantation; and her grandfather, Mingo, was a favored slave on the same plantation. The "favored" status of her grandparents allowed them, even as slaves, to be exposed to the privileged ways of life and the amenities that upper-class whites enjoyed but which were unknown to most blacks. Her grandparents, Rebecca and Mingo, aspired to that standard of living, and they passed their desire for the finer things in life on to their children. Brown's mother, the youngest child of Rebecca and Mingo, developed this desire for the best in living and education. Even with a relatively comfortable home in the middle-class section of Henderson, North Carolina, they were not satisfied with the restrictions placed on blacks in the postbellum South. They wanted more for their family and were not afraid to make the necessary sacrifices. Drawn to Massachusetts because of its progressive history in the abolitionist movement and desirous of better education and economic opportunities, the Hawkins family—nineteen in all including Charlotte's mother, grandmother, aunts, uncles, and cousins—moved from Henderson to Cambridge, Massachusetts in 1888.

In Cambridge, the family ran its own hand laundry and took in student boarders from Harvard University. Her mother, after a failed first marriage to Brown's father, remarried; and she and her new husband worked together to provide a comfortable home for the family. As one of the few black families living in Cambridge in the late nineteenth century, the Browns shared social relationships with many educated whites in the area, and they enjoyed the stimulating artistic and intellectual environment of the university town. As a young girl, Brown took piano, art, and voice lessons; attended the prestigious Cambridge English and Latin High School; and desired to attend Radcliffe for her college education. Brown's mother insisted on fine manners and on "acting like a lady," and her daughter adopted these values as her own. She was grooming herself for her goal of returning to the South and founding her own school, a challenge she had accepted early on after hearing Booker T. Washington make the plea for educated Northerners to return to the South where they were needed. And, indeed, her concern for good manners and classical education passed on to her from her family and encouraged by her New England upbringing would be important factors in helping her achieve her goals.

While sitting in a park in Cambridge reading Virgil, she was noticed by Alice Freeman Palmer, the first woman president of Wellesley College. This chance encounter led to Palmer's support of Brown's teacher training at Salem Normal School and later to Palmer's introductions to wealthy philanthropists whose support

Brown would use to build the school, which she later named for her benefactor.

The American Missionary Association representative whom Brown met on a bus ride to Cambridge from Salem, where she had been attending Salem Normal School, was also impressed with her graceful manner and her educational work. After only their first meeting, she invited Brown to teach at Bethany Institute, a small AMA school for blacks in Sedalia, North Carolina. At 19, with only one complete year of Normal School training, Brown had secured her first teaching job and a life-long opportunity to help her people.

Having used her poise and intellect to impress two individuals who would play a major role in launching her career in education, Brown became committed to the causes of education and good manners. Even though it would be a challenge for her to keep classical education and social refinement in the forefront of her educational work in the South, these elements would ultimately become the hallmarks of her success as an educator and activist.

Bethany Institute, where Brown began her career, was a small rural church school with just one teacher which operated only five months of the year. The year after Brown's arrival, the AMA decided to close schools with only one teacher, and they offered to send Brown to another school elsewhere. In her short time in Sedalia, Brown had enjoyed great support from the community; rather than have her leave, parents and community leaders volunteered to help her start her own school. It was an opportunity she had longed for since childhood. With the help of the black community in Sedalia and the support of Alice Freeman Palmer and her circle of New England friends, Brown opened Palmer Institute in 1902. It was renamed Palmer Memorial Institute when Alice Freeman Palmer died the following year.

During her years at Palmer Institute, Brown's twofold strategy for racial uplift was shaped and executed with great success as she built an institution for elementary grades through junior college that would serve the social and educational needs of the black community in Sedalia and the nation for nearly 70 years. The success of Palmer Institute, however, depended almost entirely on Brown's non-stop fund-raising, and most of the support for

Palmer Institute for the first twenty-five years came from north-ern—mostly New England and northeastern—whites.

With the encouragement of Alice Freeman Palmer bolstering their already strong sense of *noblesse oblige*, northerners contrib-uted willingly and generously to Palmer Institute. Although Brown had wanted to teach a liberal arts curriculum from the start, many northern contributors in the early years of the school had insisted that the training at Palmer be vocational and agricultural, a focus they believed more fitting for the needs of rural blacks in the South. A letter written to Brown by Frances Guthrie, a long-time supporter, is indicative: "Your pupils are not like you, they have not had your upbringings....[Do not teach] more than at their pre-sent their natures are ready to receive" (Hunter, 38).

Brown was willing to endure certain conservative sentiments in order to ensure her school's success. Even with their guarded the-ories of the role of such institutions in the lives of blacks, Northerners, at least, were convinced, as many in the South were not, of the need to assist former slaves and their dependents in achieving a better life. Brown focused her fund-raising efforts on gaining their support. In the summer, she made trips to New England and northeastern states, to make speeches, give solo con-certs, and solicit donations. She founded the Sedalia Singers at Palmer, and they too traveled the country demonstrating their tal-ents and soliciting support for the school. Brown had an impres-sive list of northern donors: Alice Freeman Palmer, Galen Stone, Charles and Frances Guthrie, Helen Kimball, John F. Townbley, and Mary Grinnel were all major contributors.[4]

For twenty years, Palmer Institute received most of its finan-cial assistance from white Northerners. After fire gutted one of the buildings in 1918, Galen Stone, a Boston businessman and broker who had been a major contributor, suggested to Brown that she should also make an appeal to Southern whites.[5] While many Northern donors believed only in Booker T. Washington's indus-trial and agricultural training for blacks (that would not take them out of their place society) they were not (as many in the South were) against the idea of the education of blacks altogether. Brown had been trying to build a school for blacks in a South that had shunned universal public education for everyone, and most especially for blacks. "Education for the whites will provide education for the Negroes" was a popular sentiment among white southerners regarding the need for black education (Hunter, 38). In the early brochures for Palmer Institute, Brown tried to allay the fears Southerners held regarding educational equality by emphasizing the school's industrial and agricultural training. "The students graduate with a practical education," boasted one brochure (Hunter, 38).

Although Brown had not entirely agreed with the philosophy and had sometimes felt constrained, she had been—publicly at least—a devoted follower of Booker T. Washington's accommodationist theory embraced by both Northern and Southern supporters. At meetings of white women's clubs where she solicited support for Palmer, for better treatment of women, and for anti-lynching legislation, she had always emphasized the helpful role that trained black women could serve in the domestic service of white women. Black women educated at Palmer, she claimed, could learn to become "fine clean mothers and good homemakers for themselves and for others" (Hunter, 39). Appealing for support from Southerners who did not see blacks as equal and who wanted no formal training for them was going to be especially difficult. When challenged by Stone to procure Southern philanthropy in greater volume, Brown knew that she would have to make a special kind of appeal.

Mammy: An Appeal to the Heart of the South, published in 1919 by Pilgrim Press of Boston, was just such an effort. And as the subtitle of the work suggests, *Mammy* was more than just a delving into the techniques of imaginative fiction. It was Brown's veiled *appeal* to Southern whites to exhibit a more obliging, appreciative stance regarding the intimate and indispensable role that blacks, most clearly exemplified in the female house slave, had served in their lives. Brown wanted to appeal to what she considered the "Christian spirit" of potential Southern white donors to the school. If they could not justify their support for Palmer Memorial Institute and justice for blacks from a standpoint of human equality, then Brown wanted to suggest that they justify it from a practical moral standpoint of duty. The unrewarded loyal servant, she believed, was the best point of departure for her entreaty. If she were to elicit their sympathy and enlist their aid, there was no more convincing standard bearer to represent her cause, she believed, than the "Black Mammy." She admitted as much in the opening paragraph of her story: "If there is any word that arouses emotion in the heart of a true Southerner, it is the word, 'Mammy'. His mind goes back to the tender embraces, the watchful eyes, the crooning melodies which lulled him to rest, the sweet old black face. 'What a memory!' he exclaims" (*Mammy*, 1).

Brown wanted to make her claim for their support of justice for blacks and the growth of Palmer Institute within the context of what white Southerners valued, even if these values were paternalistic and racist. If she could appeal to them in this way, she reasoned, then perhaps she would be successful in bringing about a change in their behavior and their thinking—a change Brown hoped would increase their support of Palmer Memorial Institute and lead the way for bettering the conditions for blacks in the South in general. Whether their redemptive offerings came in state school funding, anti-lynching legislation, or contributions to Palmer Memorial Institute, Brown wanted to emphasize the debt that whites owed to blacks for their loyal service. As Brown had warned and lamented in the introduction when she described the aging woman upon whose life the story was based, "Others enjoy the fruits of her many years of labor. She is but one of many who are left destitute in old age by those she has been faithful to unto death" (*Mammy*, viii). In recognition of what she thought was exemplary treatment of black house servants, Brown dedicated the book to Mrs. Charles Duncan McIver of Greensboro, North Carolina: "I acknowledge her personal interest in the colored members of her household and trust that many others may follow her example" (*Mammy*, viii).

The novella, only eighteen pages, tells the story of the plight of an aging black servant named Susan, who with her husband has served the white Bretherton family over a forty-year period that has included slavery, the Civil War, and beyond. Her loyalty to the family has been unquestioned; and during her time with them, she has often gone beyond what was required, even of the loyal and dutiful servant. She promises her master, when he leaves for the Civil War, that she will stay with the family until death: "Susan, take care of my wife and children, and if I never come back, stay here; if they starve, starve with them . . . if they die, die with them" (*Mammy*, 4). Even after Emancipation, which should have freed her from such promises, "Mammy," as the family calls her, feels bound to keep the promise she made to her master to serve the family until the day she dies.

Brown makes a strong case for the loyalty of Mammy. In addition to staying with the family despite her freedom, Mammy provides invaluable help to the family: "Three times a day for forty years as regular as clock work" she has gone back and forth to the house to cook the food that "the Brethertons thrived on" (*Mammy*, 5). She nurses the baby of one of the daughters who died in childbirth. Ironically, Mammy has even helped the Brethertons in their time of financial distress. When the master's business was about to fail, Mammy offered a thousand dollars of insurance payment money she had received at her son's death in order to prevent the Brethertons' financial ruin. But as Mammy ages, the Brethertons relegate her and her aging husband to a run-down cabin behind the Bretherton house. Too old now to do the cooking, Mammy is asked to sit in in order to oversee the seasoning of the meals. She is not treated with the respect and care that her years of devoted service command. She is treated as a nearly useless artifact of a time now past: the college-aged daughter of the family wants to show her college friends who visit with her at Christmas the quaint, albeit destitute, cabin that Mammy lives in, and she pleads with Mammy to bake her favorite southern biscuits to share with her friends.

Brown's choice of "Bretherton" as the last name for the white family in this story was, no doubt, a deliberate attempt on her part to remind her readers of the familial relationship that was often the reality between white families and their household servants. While there is not an indication that Mammy is related by blood to the Brethertons, it is clear that Brown wanted to suggest the possibility of blood bonds between masters and servants, and, by extension, between blacks and whites in the South. Such a suggestion would make the Brethertons' mistreatment of Mammy— and whites of blacks—even more lamentable. The sentimental literary frame of the story indicates that Brown was directing her appeal mostly to Southern white women. The women had the power, she felt, to convince white men that they should contribute to the education and social betterment of blacks. Speaking to a women's interracial conference in 1920, Brown had chided: "The Negro woman lays everything that has happened to her race at the door of the Southern white women. You can control your men" (Hunter, 41). And so it is not surprising that in the story it is Mrs. Bretherton and her step-daughter who are most sensitive to the needs of Mammy, or that it is they who are the ones who seek to enlist, albeit unsuccessfully, the aid of the husband and father: "[I]n spite of Mrs. Bretherton's desire to brush aside the thought of neglect of the two old folks who had been faithful so long, she could not wholly dismiss it" (*Mammy*, 13). They are hampered in helping Mammy and her husband, however, by Mr. Bretherton's insistence that there is no point in refurbishing the home of the aging couple: "the old folks hadn't long to live . . . it [would be] useless to spend any money on it" (*Mammy*, 12–13).

While Brown points out that the white mother and daughter are the ones most sensitive to Mammy's condition, she also points out that their feelings are only half-hearted and are of no ultimate good to Mammy if they do not follow through to see their desires fulfilled. As the narrator chides the daughter: "[L]ike most young people, it was an emotion for the moment. She went back into her world of gayety and forgot that Mammy lived" (*Mammy*, 14–15). Mammy's cruel death in the snowdrifts points vividly to the ungratefulness of the white family, and suggests the awful possibility of what could happen—indeed, what *was* happening on a symbolic level—if the right actions were not taken on behalf of those who had been good servants. In her story, Brown offered the same kind of caution, though on a much smaller scale, as Harriet Beecher Stowe had offered in *Uncle Tom's Cabin*. Like Stowe's book, Brown's story was written to point out the injustices against blacks and to appeal to a larger reading audience to change them.

In addition to utilizing the sentimental mode of fiction that appealed mainly to white women, *Mammy* also fits into the historical literary tradition of African-American women's fiction. Telling the story of slavery and servitude from the point of view of the slave woman, herself, echoed the almost unanimous character-focus in African-American women's fiction on the interior life of an African-American female protagonist. We learn Mammy's thoughts in the privacy of her own room, outside the context of the house of the slave master: "Sometimes dere ain't any wood, and sometimes dere ain't much left on the table for my old man. Things am gettin' kind o' curious. Dese here young folks ain't got no time for us. Dey jest like to p'int at us for the family's sake" (*Mammy*, 9). Though written in 1919, *Mammy* looked backwards to the contextual tradition of the slave narrative and the early focus on slave protagonists in nineteenth-century fiction by such African-American writers as Harriet Wilson in *Our Nig* and Harriet Jacobs in *Incidents in the Life of a Slave Girl*.

"Mammy": An Appeal to the Heart of the South was a demonstration of Brown's promising skill in fiction writing. Her ability to draw on the sentimental and confessional modes that revealed the horror of the system without directly attacking those responsible was a great asset in her appeal to southern whites. Readers, many of whom would identify with the Brethertons, could see and feel ashamed of their neglect and, hopefully, be changed without public ridicule. Brown had a keen understanding of the nature of race relations in the South and how many white Southerners, still aligned, psychologically at least, with the Old South planter class, related to former slaves and their descendants. Using this understanding, Brown was able to write a story that "appealed" directly to her audience's paternalistic sense of duty and loyalty—without alienating them from her larger goal of funded education for blacks. And while Brown was often criticized for her accommodationist mode and her willingness to appeal for aid and good relationships from whites within what many considered a demeaning context for blacks, she was convinced of the need for this veiled appeal. Whether through individual musical concerts, speeches, letters of solicitations, or cleverly written stories, Brown was willing to do whatever was necessary to garner continued support for social and educational reform.

Later in her life, Brown would grow weary of indirect, accommodationist appeals to whites and would speak out forthrightly about the need for justice and of rethinking the value of blacks in

American society. In the 1920s, humiliated by being forced to use Jim Crow rail accommodations after securing a Pullman berth, Brown would sue the Pullman Company. And in meetings on race relations, she would directly challenge white women to speak out against lynchings[6]: "Won't you help us friends to bring to justice the criminal element of your race...?" (Hunter, 41). Brown's short story is an example of her multifaceted use of her talents in the cause of equal education and racial uplift.

Mammy garnered little if any interest from the black press. Distribution seems to have been limited to the New England area and to southern readers in North Carolina. There were no reviews in the major black social and literary magazines.[7] Responses from many white northerners, according to the unpublished biography of Brown by Ceci Jenkins, were mixed with some feeling that the story encouraged divisiveness in the South by bringing up the old North- versus-South wounds of slavery.[8] But if the activity at Palmer after its publication is any indication, then the story's appeal to southerners was a success.[9] By 1920, Brown could report to Galen Stone that four southerners were on the school's Board of Trustees. [10] After the publication of the book, contributions to Palmer from Southern donors increased substantially. In 1922, the first brick building, Palmer Memorial Building, was constructed. Throughout the decade, Palmer began to receive subsidies from the state for its work in elementary and secondary education and the support of the American Missionary Association. Brown's appeal in her short story and the growing reputation of the work going on at the school had contributed to the growth of Palmer Institute during the 1920s and had improved race relations in the Sedalia area.

Brown's second book, *The Correct Thing To Do—To Say—To Wear*, published by Christopher House of Boston in 1941, represented the second part her strategy for racial uplift: education and refinement by blacks themselves. Since the beginning of the school's history in the early 1900s, Brown had always held a special vision for Palmer Institute. The school's motto, "educational efficiency, spiritual sincerity, and cultural security" represented the formula that Brown believed that African-American youth needed for success and acceptance. In her first twenty-five years, she had offered formal academic training and encouraged Christian ethics among her students. Because of the preferences of most of the school's donors, however, "educational efficiency" was manifested in industrial and agricultural training. The liberal arts education that Brown had preferred had not been as strongly emphasized. Students studied classical academic subjects, but they spent equal, if not more, time learning agricultural and industrial vocations and domestic home management. Brown developed in students a love for the work ethic by having them participate in the work of the school. In Sedalia, Brown carried her concern for uplifting the race beyond the classrooms. She encouraged neighbors of the school to purchase their own homes and to beautify their property. She, herself, had benefitted greatly from a classical education, hard work, and personal refinement, and she wanted her students and the Palmer community to have the same advantages. From the early 1900s to the early 1930s, the educational program at Palmer was largely based on the theory of vocational and industrial education set forth by Booker T. Washington, but Palmer graduates also had a strong sense of personal decorum and appreciation of the arts. The school served an important purpose during those early years; it was the only accredited education beyond the grammar school grades available to blacks in the Sedalia area.

During the 1930s, as a result of the Public School Movement stimulated by the Southern Education Board, public high school education became available to black students in North Carolina. The opening of public high schools took away many of Palmer's students, along with its *per capita* funds from the state. At the same time, in the aftermath of the Depression, financial contributions from both northern and southern donors were significantly reduced, and, in 1934, the AMA returned Palmer Institute to its independent status. The challenge for Brown at this time was to find a way, without her usual sources of support, to keep the school open.[11]

Brown decided that she would have to get her operating funds from the families of the students themselves. She would have to redirect the financial focus away from donors and scholarships toward the tuition dollars of those students who could afford to pay. In 1932, Brown abolished the elementary program and added junior college instruction; and she began a recruitment effort that would define a specific place for Palmer Institute in the national market of black private schools. No longer appealing solely to students in the rural South, Brown recruited blacks from around the country, including those from urban centers, who sought the rigor of a private school education and who could afford to pay the tuition. Palmer Institute moved away from its long-held position of industrial and domestic training to the kind of liberal arts curriculum that Brown had always wanted. Moreover, in order to carve out more specifically the special character of Palmer Institute in her recruiting efforts, Brown began to focus more on the "cultural security" prong of the school's three-part motto by emphasizing what she called the "social graces."[12]

She believed that if blacks did not know how to handle themselves respectably once they obtained the opportunities that they were struggling to achieve through politics and education, they would not be successful. Brown felt that etiquette was an important training area often overlooked by colleges and other schools. When reflecting on her new goals for the school, Brown lamented, "Our students are more versed in books than habits of living" (Smith and West, 197). She wanted the "New" Palmer Institute to be the banner institution focusing on character and manners. She wanted parents to know that if they desired a curriculum for their children that included training in academic subjects as well as manners and personal refinement, then Palmer Institute was the place to send them. A class in manners taught at Palmer Institute by Brown and by Amy Bailey, dean of girls in the 1930s, produced the now classic pamphlets called the "Earmarks of a Lady" and the "Earmarks of a Gentleman." The Palmer graduates were recognized as being well-trained in the social graces and the liberal arts, and within a decade, Palmer became known as the most prestigious black finishing school in the country.[13]

So widespread was Palmer's esteemed reputation that in 1940, Brown was asked to speak on the popular CBS radio program, "Wings Over Jordan," and on 10 March 1940 she delivered a speech titled "The Negro and the Social Graces." For her, it was an opportunity not only to share instruction in the social graces to a large audience of radio listeners, but also an opportunity to speak about Palmer Institute in a positive light before a national audience of potential applicants.[14] While the speech outlined prescribed rules of behavior in nearly every social setting, it also indicated clearly Brown's hopes that such behavior would ultimately serve the larger political and educational aims of blacks in American society:

> The little courtesies, the gentle voice, correct grooming; a knowledge of when to sit, when to stand; how to open and close a door; the correct attitude toward persons in authority; good manners in public places, the acquisition of these graces will go a long way in securing that recognition of ability needed to cope with human society, and will remove some of the commonest objections to our presence in large numbers.
>
> Let us take time, therefore, to be gracious, to be thoughtful, to be kind, using the social graces as one means of turning the wheels of progress with greater velocity on the upward road to equal opportunity and justice for all (Marteena, 73–74).

The speech was full of condescending phrases that caused leaders like Du Bois to call Brown's a "voice for the white South"; but for most of those who listened, the speech was a great success and was subsequently printed in a leaflet published by the Commission on Interracial Cooperation in Atlanta.[15] After her appearance on the CBS radio program, Brown was asked to edit a weekly column in the *Norfolk Journal and Guide* on etiquette called the "Correct Thing," and she became sought after as a lecturer at many schools throughout the country. As a result of these publications and appearances, Brown became known as the "First Lady of Social Graces." Because of this groundswell of interest in manners and social rules, she published independently *The Correct Thing To Do—To Say—To Wear* in 1940. In 1941, it was reissued by The Christopher Publishing House of Boston.[16] On a practical level, the book represented the culmination of the shift in educational focus at Palmer Memorial Institute that began in the late 1930s. On a more philosophical level, it was a symbolic testament to the kind of manners-first-the-rest-will-follow idea of achievement that Brown had struggled for all of her life.

The Correct Thing is a small encyclopedia of manners combining the rules of etiquette Brown learned from her mother and from teachers at Palmer Institute, as well as those agreed upon by other experts such as Emily Post, Anna Richards, and Margery Wilson. It seems more a book of the early 1900s than the 1940s, with its emphasis on Victorian morality. But its popularity indicated that many blacks were still striving to overcome negative stereotypes, and they were interested in finding ways of acceptance. Furthermore, like many Americans—they desired the comfort and ease in social settings that Brown's book promised; they wanted to be sure that they were doing the "correct thing." The book was a handy little manual that outlined what was considered to be proper behavior in nearly every social situation. Brown numbered all the rules, with hopes that students would learn them as a kind of social catechism that would become a part of their daily living. As she pointed out in the introduction, she hoped the book would enable students to do the correct thing with ease:

> This little book which I send forth out of years of experience and observation is not intended to put one on his guard in company but rather to help one to know and practice the art of kindness, the art of graciousness, the art of expressing one's best self when alone, thus developing the habit of doing the correct thing without effort or apparent notice. (*Correct*, vii)

The book went through five printings and won the Mark Twain Society Book Award in 1944. It became the "text on manners" at Palmer Institute and was used by many schools and social clubs throughout the country. It was revised for present-day use in 1965. The striking thing about the text is its meticulous attention to the smallest detail of behavior. The chapter outlining proper behavior at home instructs young readers not to "get up in the morning with a grouch and [to] always greet each member of the family with a cheerful 'good morning'" (*Correct*, 48). It cautions young homemakers on everything from how far down to pull the window shades to where to hang certain articles of clothing to dry.

Beyond the home, the book carries instructions for the proper social graces and expected behavior to be exercised at meal times, at school, at church, at concerts, at the theater, at the movies, in dance halls, at weddings, on dates, on weekend visits, and on the telephone. It provides "how tos" on travel, table settings, invitations, introductions, and even includes a conceding section on the proper behavior when smoking entitled "If You Must Indulge."

The book also includes her now famous lists describing the "Earmarks of a Lady" and the "Earmarks of a Gentleman." "A Lady," Brown outlines in numbered precision:

> 1. Is polite when entering or leaving a room. 2. Passes behind people. 3. Answers and comes when called by teacher or parent. 4. Graciously answers, 'Yes, Miss A,' when called or 'No, Mrs. B,' should the reply require such. 5. Uses, Please and thank you. 6. Keeps hands off of other people. 7. Does not chew gum in public. 8. Awaits her turn. 9. Closes doors quietly. . . ." (*Correct*, 48–49).

The list continues to include twenty-four do's and don'ts for ladies. For the men, there are only eleven dos and don'ts but they are just as specific. A gentleman is a man who: "1. Maintains and exhibits genuine respect for women, 2. Is careful to call a person's name when addressing him, and to say 'Thank you....' 3. Avoids making an unnecessary 'scene' under any circumstances, 4. Does not use profane language or tell questionable jokes," and true to the Palmer tradition for both ladies and men, a gentleman "opens and closes doors noiselessly and leaves them as he found them" (*Correct*, 106–7).

The Correct Thing became the bible of manners for generations of students at Palmer Institute and became the primer for African-American youth at other schools who wanted to behave properly. It seems, in retrospect, to have been a restrictive book, particularly appearing as it did near the middle of the twentieth century. But the codes and expectations outlined were indicative of the kind of behavior that was expected in black households and in black institutions during the area of segregation in the South. The book shows the lengths that black youth and their parents were willing to go in order to achieve and maintain respectability. And while many of the rules were taught by Brown and others in order to gain respect from those outside their communities, the codes were eventually appropriated by the black communities for themselves and became the codes of behavior for every generation of black youth.

Throughout her life, Charlotte Hawkins Brown worked steadfastly for the cause of social and economic uplift for African Americans. Although in later years, critics have thought *The Correct Thing* was too condescending, the book was representative of what Brown believed constituted the all-important edge for blacks in improving their relationships with whites and in convincing them of their right to equality. The book provided a common reference point where agreed-upon rules for social behavior were documented for use by parents and teachers throughout the country. The expectations outlined in some of the areas of the book, particularly those in the section "Earmarks of a Lady" seem to be in sharp contradiction to the way even Brown, herself, lived her public life. As Tera W. Hunter has pointed out, Brown surely did not always "wait her turn," and wasn't always "passive"; but she did have the knowledge of what was required to educate the whole person, and she wanted the mission of Palmer Institute to be the cultivation of well-educated and well-mannered individuals for the society. "Acquire manners;" Brown said many times, and "the rest will come" (Smith and West, 205). This had been the example of her own life; there was no reason for her not to believe that it could also serve as the example for others.

Charlotte Hawkins Brown retired as president of Palmer Memorial Institute in 1952. She continued working for the school and for the cause of racial justice until she died on January 11, 1961. She had lived a lifetime of working in a variety of arenas of racial justice and social uplift. Her greatest contribution, however, was the legacy of Palmer Memorial Institute. In her race and educational work, as historians have concluded, Brown might have been too hopeful in her thoughts that whites would support indefinitely and in great numbers the cause of blacks solely on the basis of blacks' demonstrations of self-refinement and of whites' feelings of *noblesse oblige*. But Charlotte Brown's steadfastness in wielding this double edged sword in order to uplift the race was unwavering. With this approach, she built an institution that served her people from 1902 to 1970, when it closed its doors. But while education and refinement had gotten her the initial attention and the continuing support to build Palmer Institute, Brown learned, as a younger generation of African-American students would also learn, that it would take more than education and social graces and the good will of whites to change the restrictive conditions under which blacks lived. As the Civil Rights Movement was to demonstrate later, it would take definitive legal action as well.

We must see both these works, then, as self-conscious attempts to achieve practical and political aims. The resurgence of interest in these writings, particularly *The Correct Thing*, in later years has suggested that the practical, if not political, needs of self-improvement and gracious manners have had lasting value among African Americans. Many of the "how tos" outlined in *The Correct Thing* continue to be the pivot points for judging good manners in African-American households even today.

Had Brown continued the imaginative writing began in *Mammy: An Appeal to the Heart of the South*, she might have expanded her abilities in the genre of sentimental fiction to which she seemed, (at least publicly), to have been drawn; or, she might have developed more fully her promising beginning in exploring the psychological interior of African-American women's lives. With her varied experiences working among African-American women in teaching, fund-raising, and community work, she would have added much to our understanding of the inner thoughts of African-American women in many walks of life.

But in the context of Brown's political and professional life, the larger aim of these two books went beyond exercises in the artistry of writing fiction or in the drafting of a code of manners for purely social aims. These two books, like Palmer Institute and her work for racial justice, are testaments to Brown's faith in the ultimate sense of justice and good will on the part of whites and in her belief in the social and intellectual potential of her people. Bolstered by the climate in which she grew up, Brown believed that with a supportive rather than prohibitive attitude by whites and with educational and social readiness by blacks, her larger goal of uplift for the first generation out of slavery and their children could be achieved. These books represent her willingness to go beyond the "leg-work" of club meetings, letter writing, concerts, teaching, and speaking to achieve respect and justice for her race. They represent her belief in the power of the printed word—the narrative or the documented guide—in changing attitudes of whites and instructing blacks in educational and social uplift, both of which she believed were necessary to remove the restrictive conditions under which blacks lived in the South during the first half of the twentieth century.

BIBLIOGRAPHY

Brown, Charlotte Hawkins. *The Correct Thing To Do—To Say—To Wear*. Sedalia, NC: published by the author, 1940.

———. *Mammy: An Appeal to the Heart of the South*. Boston: Pilgrim Press, 1919.

———. "Cooperation Between White and Colored Women." *Missionary Review* 45 (June 1922): 484–87.

Hunter, Tera. " 'The Correct Thing': Charlotte Hawkins Brown and the Palmer Institute." *Southern Exposure* 11, no. 5 (September/October 1983): 37–43.

Marteena, Constance. *The Lengthening Shadow of a Woman: A Biography of Charlotte Hawkins Brown*. Hicksville, New York: Exposition Press, 1977.

The National Union Catalog Pre-1956 Imprints. Vol. 78. Chicago: Mansell, 1970.

Smith, Sandra and Earle West. "Charlotte Hawkins Brown." *Journal of Negro Education* 51, no. 3 (1982): 191–206.

Thompson, Kathleen. "Charlotte Hawkins Brown." *Black Women in American History: The Twentieth Century*. Ed. Darlene Clark Hine, 172–74. Brooklyn, NY: Carlson Publishing, 1990.

Tillman, Elvena. "Charlotte Hawkins Brown." *Dictionary of American Negro Biography*. Ed. Rayford Logan and Michael Winston, 65–67. New York: Norton, 1982.

Vick, Marsha. "Charlotte Hawkins Brown." In *Notable Black American Women*, ed. Jessie Carney Smith, 109–14. Detroit: Gale Research, Inc., 1992.

NOTES

[1]Constance Hall Marteena, *The Lengthening Shadow of a Woman: A Biography of Charlotte Hawkins Brown* (Hicksville, New York: Exposition Press, 1977), 95; hereafter cited in text as Marteena. Biographical information for this introduction comes from Marteena as well as the following sources: Tera Hunter, " 'The Correct Thing': Charlotte Hawkins Brown and the Palmer Institute," *Southern Exposure* 11, no. 5 (September/October 1983): 37–43, hereafter cited in text as Hunter; Sandra Smith and Earle West, "Charlotte Hawkins Brown," *Journal of Negro Education* 51, No. 3 (1982): 191–206, hereafter cited in text as Smith and West; Kathleen Thompson, "Charlotte Hawkins Brown," in *Black Women in American History, The Twentieth Century*, ed. Darlene Clark Hine (Brooklyn, NY: Carlson Publishing, 1990), 172–74; Elvena Tillman, "Charlotte Hawkins Brown," in *Dictionary of American Negro Biography*, ed. Rayford Logan and Michael Winston (New York: Norton, 1982), 65–67; Marsha Vick, "Charlotte Hawkins Brown," *Notable Black American Women*, ed. Jessie Carney Smith (Detroit: Gale Research, Inc., 1992), 109–14.

[2]It is my preference to capitalize the words "Black" and "White" when they refer to people, but they are lowercased here in order to be consistent with the publisher's house style.

[3]Charlotte Hawkins Brown, *Mammy: An Appeal to the Heart of the South* (Boston: Pilgrim Press, 1919), hereafter cited in text as *Mammy*; Charlotte Hawkins Brown, *The Correct Thing To Do—To Say—To Wear* (Sedalia, NC: published by the author, 1940), hereafter cited in text as *Correct*. Page numbers given in citations to these two works refer to the original edition, facsimiles of which are reproduced in the present volume.

[4]For a full discussion of the contributions made by various northern donors, see Marteena, 36–37, 53–59; Smith and West, 194–95.

[5]Marteena and Smith and West rely on letters between Stone and Brown on file at the Schlesinger Library at Radcliffe College in their discussion of Stone's requests. See Marteena, 54–55 and Smith and West, 194–95.

[6]In addition to the comments documented in Tera Hunter's essay, there is also evidence of Brown's open appeal to white women against lynching in her essay June 1922 essay in the *Missionary Review*, "Cooperation Between White and Colored Women," 484–87.

[7]I examined every issue of *Crisis* and *Opportunity* from 1918 through 1924 and found no reviews of *Mammy*.

[8]See Smith and West, 200.

[9]Smith and West, Marteena, and others have also pointed out that southerners became more sympathetic to Brown's work after the fire in 1917 that gutted the industrial building on campus.

[10]See Smith and West, 194; Marteena, 53–54; and Vick, 111.

[11]See Hunter's discussion of Brown's effort to get money for the school mainly from tuition-paying students, 40.

[12]For discussion of the shifting focus at Palmer in the 1940s see Hunter, 39–40; Smith and West, 193; and Marteena, 71–72.

[13]Conversations with individuals who attended high school and college during the 1940s and 1950s support this claim. See also Hunter, 40; Vick, 111; and Tillman, 65.

[14]For the text of the speech Brown delivered on the "Wings over Jordan" Program, see Marteena, 72–74.

[15]Quoted in Hunter, 40.

[16]*The National Union Catalog* for publications prior to 1956 lists two entries for *The Correct Thing*. The 1940 entry is presumed to be Brown's independent publishing effort, and the 1941 entry lists the publisher as Christopher House of Boston.

"MAMMY"

"Mammy"

AN APPEAL TO THE HEART
OF THE SOUTH

BY
CHARLOTTE HAWKINS BROWN

Price $1.00 net

Copyright 1919
By CHARLOTTE HAWKINS BROWN

THE PILGRIM PRESS
BOSTON

[2]

An Appeal to the Heart of the South

DEDICATED TO MY GOOD FRIEND

𝕸𝖗𝖘. 𝕮𝖍𝖆𝖘. 𝕯𝖚𝖓𝖈𝖆𝖓 𝕸𝖈𝕴𝖛𝖊𝖗

GREENSBORO, NORTH CAROLINA

IT IS WITH GRATITUDE I ACKNOWLEDGE HER
PERSONAL INTEREST IN THE COLORED MEM-
BERS OF HER HOUSEHOLD AND TRUST THAT
MANY OTHERS MAY FOLLOW HER EXAMPLE

CHARLOTTE HAWKINS BROWN

PALMER MEMORIAL INSTITUTE
SEDALIA, NORTH CAROLINA

Introduction

*This story is based upon the
following incident:*

On a farm near Sedalia died a
wealthy spinster who had passed
her allotted number of summers.
There survived her a faithful colored servant, "Granny Polly,"
who for more than a half century
had answered to every beckon and
call, from gardener to housemaid.
This "Mammy" lived within a few
feet of the back door of her
"Charge" in a makeshift cabin,
the last left from a group of
homes used for slave quarters.

Among the many large and
gracious bequests left to distant
relatives and friends, "Mammy"
received the handsome legacy of
twenty-five dollars.

She, now past eighty, is still digging in the garden of a grandchild who gave her shelter. Her best days are gone. Others enjoy the fruits of her many years of labor.

She is but one of many who are left destitute in old age by those she has been faithful to unto death.

"Mammy"

F there is any word that arouses emotion in the heart of a true Southerner, it is the word, "Mammy." His mind goes back to the tender embraces, the watchful eyes, the crooning melodies which lulled him to rest, the sweet old black face. "What a memory!" he exclaims.

.　　.　　.　　.　　.

The old cabin leaning far towards the rising sun told that its day was far spent. Here and there, a sill seemed held up by a post, one end of which was buried deep in the ground about eight or ten feet away from the

[1]

flint rock foundation—a true relic
of slavery days.

It was the only one of its kind
in the neighborhood, but the land
on which it stood was eyed by
real estate dealers and owners
who vied with each other as to
the purchase of this extraordina-
rily valuable piece of property.
The yard had a look of desolation
and neglect, yet the sweet-scented
magnolias, roses and syringas, now
almost covered with vines, told
that long ago a lover of art and
beauty had lent a charm to this
now forlorn hovel.

The back yard of the cabin
opened into the back yard of a
regal looking mansion, once the
home of one of Virginia's prominent governors. Its stately, mas-
sive columns gave it the style
and dignity of architecture re-

[2]

moved a hundred years from the twentieth century. This spacious residence was occupied by the fourth or fifth generation of the Brethertons, the mere mention of whose name gave tone and color to any picture of social life in Virginia. Like many of their kind, the Brethertons had fought and lost, and all that was left to them after the sixties were the home and the name which made a Bretherton hold his head high even though his feet were bare.

The Brethertons had been compelled to sell, acre by acre, the large farm on which a thousand or more negroes had spent days of toil. Costly residences now enclosed them, until only Aunt Susan and her "Ole Man," as she called him, could point to the

[3]

Gramley Library
Salem College
Winston-Salem, NC 27108

spot that marked the slave quarters fifty years before.

Aunt Susan had been the "Mammy" of the family for years before the war. She loved to recall the words of old Colonel Bretherton, who said to her as the last man of the family joined the Confederate army, to bind closer the chains that held her people: "Susan, take care of my wife and children, and if I never come back, stay here; if they starve, starve with them . . . if they die, die with them."

The old Colonel never returned, and though Aunt Susan heard the voice of freedom calling to her a few years afterwards, she had given her word to the Colonel and she kept it until the day of her death.

The "ole man" had been

[4]

Colonel's body-guard. It was he who brought the news of Colonel's death; his own strong arm had borne the fainting Mistress to the couch of down, but now he sat by the fireside in the old cabin, a paralytic, scarcely able to help himself.

Three times a day for forty years as regular as a clock, dear Aunt Susan went back and forth to the "white folks'" house, and cooked the food that the Brethertons thrived on.

The sons grew to manhood and married. Their children and their children's children climbed up on Mammy's knee, nursed often from Mammy's bosom, for one daughter had given her life to give to the world a new life, and this new life lived and thrived from blood of Mammy's blood,

[5]

flesh of Mammy's flesh. This child called "Edith," because she was the image of her girl mother, Edith, always seemed "near" to Mammy. She was now a young "Miss" at Boarding School, and Mammy's famous beaten biscuits always adorned her lunch when she was leaving, and were never missing from the Thanksgiving box. Then, there was something so historically romantic about the reference when Edith could say to the girls, "My dear old black Mammy baked the biscuits just for me. She's been a servant in our family for forty years or more." This statement carried with it a degree of aristocracy that only a Southerner can appreciate.

Mammy had long ago laid to rest her own little babe, as she

[6]

[14]

always spoke of him, although he had grown to manhood long before. He had offered her a home and every comfort in the North; she preferred the cabin, it seemed—no, it was not the cabin, for ofttimes, on bitter cold nights when the winds would whistle, she would kneel and ask God to be a foundation for the old cabin, until the coming of another day, for each moment she thought it would rock its last time. But, ah, the solemn promise to the Colonel, "till I die!"

Mammy was getting old and rheumatism had set in, so the "white folks" had to get a younger woman to do the cooking, but she must be on hand to do the seasoning, because a Bretherton would not eat a meal at Stone Ledge, as the old Man-

[7]

sion was called, unless Mammy had a hand in it.

The days went by wearily for Mammy's "ole man," but the sweet patience with which the loyal soul watched over him was beautifully pathetic. "Ole Missus don't come no more to see us, and de young 'uns has forgotten us," he thought.

The old ties of former days had been broken between him and the friends of his own race; they had moved away. New folks who had no interest in him had come to town. Sometimes Mammy would find him helpless at the wood pile where he had presumed upon the strength of his one good side to lighten her burden to get the wood.

"Ole man," she would say, "I don' tole you to stay in de house

[8]

and let me wait on you; you done
been faithful to me and de white
folks for many a year, and dere
ain't no use in frettin' 'cause you
ain't young and spry." And
Mammy would heave a sigh, for
growing signs of neglect had
weighed heavily on her, since old
Mrs. Bretherton hadn't been able
to get around.

"Sometimes dere ain't any wood,
and sometimes dere ain't much
left on the table for my old man.
Things am gettin' kind o' curious.
Dese here young folks ain't got
no time for us. Dey jest like to
p'int at us for the family's sake,"
thought she, but to encourage
"Pappy," as she sometimes called
him, she spoke out in jolly tones,
"Go long, Pappy, 'twice a child
an' once a man,' Colonel used to
say; and I 'spec' you's done

[9]

reached dat second childhood. You want dese young 'uns running down here a-climbin' on your knees like dey use to," and she turned her face to hide the tears. "We'se been faithful; dese hands hab nursed ebry child in dat Bretherton family. I'se laid 'em on my lap and hugged 'em to my breast,—lors a mussy, I lubs dem children, but little Miss Edith is the only one that thinks enough of Mammy to come down here to de old cabin and see how we-uns is libin'."

"Bless ma soul, Christmas is coming, and I looks for her like robins do the spring; she brings sunshine," said Pappy.

Miss Edith came home, bringing some of her friends from the North who attended St. Mary's school—one of the most select

[10]

boarding-schools in the country. She wanted to give them a taste of a Southern Christmas.

The very interesting course in sociology in school had attacked the cabin life in which the white people had forced the negroes to live, and Edith had become popular by telling of her beloved Mammy, and how she had found shelter within reach of them for forty years, how her mother, grandmother and great-grandmother had cared for her and met her every need. Everybody had warmed up to Edith because of this interesting account of "negro fidelity" and "white devotion."

Hardly had Edith exchanged greetings with the home folks before she realized that it would be perfectly natural for the girls

[11]

to want to see this beautiful picture of service and gratitude. She began to talk it over with her mother (by the way, this mother was a new one whom Edith's father had chosen for her long before Mammy had given up her claim to be the child's sole guardian).

"Mother," said Edith, "it would never do to carry the girls down to the 'ole cabin.' I know it's spotless, but it looks as if it would tumble down every minute, and when I was there last fall, Mammy had a wash tub on top of the bed to catch the large drops of rain."

"Why didn't you tell your papa?" said her mother.

"Mother," Edith answered, "I did, but papa said the old folks hadn't long to live, and as soon as they were dead the cabin would

[12]

[20]

be torn down and the property would be for sale, and he said it was useless to spend any money on it."

"Well, don't let the situation worry you, little girl," remarked her mother, "your friends will be having such a gay time that the question of sociology in these quarters will not enter their thoughts."

But in spite of Mrs. Bretherton's desire to brush aside the thought of neglect of the two old folks who had been faithful so long, she could not wholly dismiss it.

"Listen, Edith," said her mother, "we ought to do more for Mammy. This winter when your papa's business was about to fail, Mammy somehow or other noticed that something had hap-

[13]

pened. It was really necessary to cut down the food supply. She sought the confidence of your grandmother, who loves Mammy as a sister, you know; Granny told her all. Edith, it would have brought tears to your eyes if you had seen them weeping on each other's shoulders. I saw Granny count out ten one hundred dollar bills that Mammy handed to her which she said she had kept as her son's ' 'surance money.'

"We all thought that boy worthless. I could not understand, but I followed Mammy to the back door. I saw her look towards heaven as she said earnestly, 'Till I die.' "

The tears trickled down Edith's cheeks, but like most young people, it was an emotion for the

[14]

moment. She went back into her world of gayety and forgot that Mammy lived.

The holidays came to a close with a blinding snowstorm.

Early in the morning of January sixth, Mammy rose and peeped out, to see the snow piled up high. "Pappy," she called, "Mammy's child leaves dis morning, and ain't nary beaten biscuit dere to put in her lunch. Dese hands ain't never failed dat child, and de snow ain't going to make dem fail dis mornin'."

Pappy sighed. "Mammy, white folks don't care long for us lak dey used to—we's gettin' old and no 'count."

She protested, however, dressing in the meantime. She pried the door open, while a mass of snow fell on the inside. The wind

[15]

whistled. Bundled up in a shawl, she sought the garden gate, but just as the gate clicked, an avalanche of snow from the roof of Stone Ledge fell, burying beneath it all that was in its path.

An impatient little girl wondered why Mammy didn't come to give her the beaten biscuits.

Late in the afternoon, Pappy grew weary of waiting and watching for her who never stayed away so long. Eating the bread and milk which she always provided for his breakfast did not satisfy him for the day. Soon a whistle, and then a young man rushed into the cabin crying, "Mammy, Mammy, come quick, Grandma is dead."

But no Mammy answered.

Pappy, excited, hobbled to the door just in time to see the snow

[16]

melting. The red bandanna of his mate of fifty years told the story. "Until I die!" She had kept her vow to the last. He swooned to the floor, and how long he lay there no one knows.

Green Hill Cemetery is a beautiful place, and the most prominent in it is marked by a monument of a soldier in uniform—the "Colonel."

Here his good wife's remains were laid to rest amidst the funeral rites of Church and state.

A new board marked the last resting-place of "Mammy," to which she journeyed in the county wagon.

Outside the County Home, occasionally, is seen an old man counting his years into a century, who murmurs unceasingly: "White folks don't care long for

[17]

us lak dey use to—we's gettin'
ole and no 'count."

A sign "For Sale" marks the
place where Mammy once lived.

Each year the Brethertons
make a pilgrimage to Green Hill
Cemetery to plant flowers, but
only the kind honeysuckle creeps
over the grave of the body in
ebony whose soul was whiter than
snow.

THE CORRECT THING

"*Manners must adorn knowledge and smooth its way in the world; without them it is like a great rough diamond, very well in a closet by way of curiosity, and also for its intrinsic value; but most prized when polished.*"

I have to live with myself and so
I want to be fit for myself to know.

I want to be able as days go by
Always to look myself straight in the eye.
I don't want to stand with the setting sun
And hate myself for the things I've done.

The Correct Thing

To Do -
To Say -
To Wear

By

CHARLOTTE HAWKINS BROWN

SEDALIA, N. C.
PUBLISHED BY THE AUTHOR
1940

COPYRIGHT, 1940, BY
CHARLOTTE HAWKINS BROWN

PRICE: ONE DOLLAR

PRINTED IN THE UNITED STATES OF AMERICA, BY
THE SEEMAN PRINTERY, INC., DURHAM, N. C.

DEDICATED

TO

THE YOUTH OF AMERICA

IN MEMORY OF

MY MOTHER

CAROLINE FRANCES WILLIS

INTRODUCTION

Dear Friend:

"Of the making of books there is no end." Then why should another book of etiquette be added to the scores of those already on the market? Out of the hearts of a humble people has come the desire for recognition of those vital qualities of soul which they feel and cultivate from time to time, but are thwarted in their attempt to express for lack of the knowledge of the best means of expression. I write in answer to the hundreds of questions asked me by my own students, for many of my associates who give evidence of much learning without ease in their social approach to life.

The practice of fine manners is an art, but it should always be so natural that there be nothing of affectation about it. The habit of being one's best self daily in the little courtesies at home, to those nearest to one, so establishes the individual's expression of fine and gracious personality that meeting a stranger at any time has, for him or her, neither fear nor dread.

This little book which I send forth out of years of experience and observation is not intended to put one on his guard in company but rather to help one to know and practice the art of kindness, the art of graciousness, the art of expressing one's best self when alone, thus developing the habit of doing the correct thing without effort or apparent notice.

Some people are born with charm, that essential, airy, indescribable something without which all else sinks into insignificance in an attempt to establish in any measure our place in human society. However feminine the word "charm" in its essence, no man feels underrated when he is said to possess a personality of great charm.

This book offers no miracles for sudden metamorphosis. It does, however, set down certain definite principles upon which charm depends and by the practice of which a more desirable and pleasing personality may be achieved.

One studies to become efficient in music, versed in literature, and accepted in art. Versatility adds to one's ability to entertain, makes one more sought after and gives greater satisfaction to one's self in the larger activities that go to make up happy wholesome living. It adds greatly to one's admirers. So it is with the natural and unaffected practice of the social graces, little courtesies which combine thoughtfulness of others and forgetfulness of self into a unified and unconscious effort we create an atmosphere of happiness and contentment in pursuit of those things which keep life always on a high level.

I, therefore, offer my gratitude to the many friends of my childhood in the New England area who, in schools and homes teeming with cultural atmosphere, gave me an opportunity to observe the fine art of living.

To my mother first who taught me as a child in her own way, to be kind, polite and generous under all conditions and circumstances; to my teachers in the English High School at Cambridge, Massachusetts, who met the established attitude with greater interest in developing it to a higher level; to the inspiring and helpful friendship of Mrs. Osborn W. Bright, Mrs. Charles M. Connfelt, and Mrs. Charles S. Guthrie, all of New York City, who for more than twenty-five years gave themselves so untiringly in fellowship and understanding in the shaping of the ideals and policies of the cultural life of this institution; to the warm sympathetic interest of that first friend in this vicinity, who expressed belief in the possibility of achieving nobler ends for a minority group, Mrs. Charles D. McIver, of Greensboro, North Carolina; to Mrs. Galen L. Stone, of Brookline, Massachusetts, for her personal friendship through the years and her appreciation of my every endeavor to set up high standards without regard to race or creed evidenced in the large financial support given me; to the members of the faculty of the Palmer Memorial Institute, present and past, who have assisted in such research as was necessary to answer the many questions so persistently asked by our students.

Finally, but not less gratefully, I acknowledge the painstaking effort at research into the records of the teachings of the Palmer Memorial Institute, its established code of ethics, the various assembly and chapel talks, the quiet hours of discussion, the social program and the subsequent compilation and arrangement of this material by my assistant and collaborator, *Miss Cecie R. Jenkins,* without whose devoted service and continuing enthusiasm this effort might not have been achieved.

Sincerely yours,

CHARLOTTE HAWKINS BROWN.

CONTENTS

THE CORRECT THING

CHAPTER I

AT HOME

As are families, so is society. If well ordered, well instructed, and well governed, they are the springs from which go forth the streams of national greatness and prosperity—of civil order and public happiness.—THAYER.

So many young people have a peculiar idea of what should be the conduct in the home. To them home is the place where one disregards all semblance of courtesy and culture, where concern for the rights and comforts of others is of minor significance, where the individual centers his attention primarily upon his personal desires, likes and dislikes, regardless of the remaining members of the household. It is to be remembered, on the contrary, that home should be a center of mutual love and interest, of genuine respect and esteem, and a school for developing and practicing the fine art of manners, speech and attitudes so willingly and lavishly bestowed upon outsiders. One naturally receives more devotion and loving attention at home than anywhere else; therefore in a thousand little ways you may show your gratitude and appreciation by being at your best at all times and under all circumstances.

Of course there will come in a home some disagreements and arguments, for seldom do any two persons think alike. But it is better to admit that you are likely to be in error, even when you think you are right, than put rancor and hurt in the heart of a member of the family by such assertions as "You are wrong" or "You don't know what you are talking about." A better or finer thing to say when one sees an argument getting the better of one's judgment is "Suppose we give ourselves a little time to think this over and get more facts on the subject."

Never permit yourself to leave the family table or living room at the close of the day angry or displeased. No one can measure the hurt of a parent who does not hear the accustomed sweet, "goodnight" or feel the touch of tenderness of a goodnight kiss when he or she has been misunderstood, even though parents unintentionally sometimes make grave errors in speech and argument.

What are, then, some of the little thoughtful acts that help to make home really a "Home Sweet Home?"

1. Don't get up in the morning with a "grouch." Always greet each member of the family with a cheerful "good morning," and maintain a sunny disposition throughout the day.

2. When you are going out, let someone know where you may be found and when you may be expected to return. You never can tell what will happen and you may be needed.

3. Do your part in answering the door bell or telephone. Don't always wait for the other person to do it.

4. Don't leave the sections of the family newspaper scattered or turned inside out when you finish reading it. Put the various parts together so that the next person can easily find and handle them.

5. Don't mistake a family bathroom for a private bath. Every other person has the same right to use it that you have.

6. Don't monopolize the radio. Your favorite program may conflict with the favorite of someone else. Be agreeable and take turns.

7. Offer your assistance in whatever work needs to be done. Don't think that you just can't wash dishes be-

cause you are a boy or you would not dare clean up the front yard because you are a girl.

8. Don't save your table manners until company comes. You and your family are just as good and deserve just as much consideration as any of your friends or acquaintances.

9. *Be saving.* Don't burn lights unnecessarily. Be sure that the hot water faucet is turned off. Don't leave the hose on too long in the back yard. Don't drive the automobile around the corner when you can walk. Don't turn the radio on in the morning and let it run all day. Don't leave the outside doors wide open when the furnace is going full blast.

10. Remember that your parents have done more for you than anyone else in the world. Always accord them the greatest respect and attention under all circumstances.

11. Go occasionally with mother and father, brother and sister to a movie or dance. They are good company also.

12. Buy mother a box of handkerchiefs and father a new tie when you get your allowance. They will appreciate it thoroughly.

13. Think just as much of your home and your home folks as you do of any other place or people.

14. Do not leave clothes, books, trash, toys, etc. lying around. When you have finished using them, return them to their proper places.

15. Respect each person's private property. Do not read mail, go into or borrow personal things without asking permission.

16. Do not continue to talk about what the other people have in their homes or how fine the food is on Johnnie's table or in Mary's lunch when you know those

in the home are putting forth their best effort to please and satisfy you.

17. Remember that a little praise, an occasional compliment in appreciation of an effort made in your behalf, brings more joy to the heart of the giver than any expensive gift or amount of money you can bestow.

18. Don't make too much of public affection. It will seem more showy than sincere.

19. A gentle "Yes, Mother," "No, Daddy," pulling mother's chair from the table, holding *her* coat and helping Dad on with *his,* a ready whisk broom for any extraneous lint that may have gotten on the coat or dress overnight will be expressions of love and interest most gratifying.

20. Never permit any older member of the family to open a door if you are near it.

21. Never take your seat at the table while Mother is standing unless she excuses you.

22. Never permit Mother or the woman at the head of the house to take more steps than necessary to give you service. In families where there are no maids, children may easily take turns at waiting on the table.

23. Always wipe your feet at the door to avoid the extra work made necessary by deposits from your shoes.

24. Always place your wet umbrella in the stand where there is usually a metal holder to catch the dripping water. In the event there is no such article, any convenient place will do where the water will not mar the furniture.

25. Do not deposit open tin cans or even pasteboard boxes in the garbage cans for it entails extra and disagreeable effort on the part of the housekeeper or maid before putting it out for city disposal.

26. Do not pull down the shades to the window ledge. The lighting is part of the beauty of the home and, seen

from the outside, gives evidence of cheer, comfort and pleasure. (Be sure to carefully adjust the shades in your bedrooms and use dim lights when getting ready to retire, for shadows cast on cloth shades make many pictures upon which out-siders may gaze.)

27. Don't hang clothes or put polished shoes in your windows to dry. They make an ugly sight for passersby.

28. Don't yell out of the windows to give messages across the lawn or to hail passersby. The only exception to this is in isolated homes or on farms in the country where custom accepts.

29. Young man, don't possess the family automobile. Larking and joy-riding may be all right, if not over-indulged, and taking the best girl for a ride has its glamour. But the rest of the family have made an investment in this commodity also and ought to share whatever joy its possession can give.

30. Don't wear one another's clothes, however intimate the members of the family may be. Clothes have distinct personality and, however attractive, may show the one for whom it was not bought up to a disadvantage.

31. Whatever else happens, in order to keep home happy, don't be a combatant. You may be smart and you may be the only one in the family that has a B. S., but the rest of the family may have been somewhere too and seen a few things and possess that most uncommon of all common things—common sense and discretion. Truly learned people are the last to parade their knowledge at the disparagement of those who are less advantaged.

It seems to be a human weakness to take relatives and close friends too much for granted. Few persons willfully neglect or show disrespect for them. Lack of thought can be blamed for most of this. The more closely we weave into the fabric of our most intimate home life the finesse of decorum and the cheerfulness of attitude that is often wrongly reserved for mere acquaintances, the more surely can we make of our homes beautiful havens of joy and contentment.

CHAPTER II

AT MEALTIME

The chief pleasure in eating does not consist in costly season-
ing or exquisite flavor, but in yourself.—HORACE.

One of the primary things to remember about a meal is
that its purpose is not solely to provide the body with
needed food. Each meal should foster a fellowship expressed in fitting conversation among the persons at the
table. It should also, through the preparation of food and
arrangement of service, create an atmosphere that appeals
to the eye as well as to the taste. If the partaking of food
were the only aim, there would be no need for sparkling
glassware and painted china, shining silver and fresh linen,
attractively decorated dining rooms and white-aproned
waitresses. But all of these things unite together to form a
setting conducive to harmonious social intercourse and a
thorough appreciation of tasty food.

For the smooth running, beauty and real enjoyment of
any meal there are certain general rules that must be ob-
served. In as concise form as possible, they are these.

1. Always arrive at a meal at the appointed time.
2. Young men, draw back the chair for the girl or woman
   next to you, push it under her as she sits down and
   then take your seat.
3. Sit with your knees together and both feet on the floor,
   not on the rounds of the chair or wrapped around the
   legs.
4. Keep up an interesting conversation in which all persons at the table are included.

5. Avoid lounging. Keep your spine straight, your body poised a little forward and your mind occupied with the conversation you are helping to make pleasant.

6. Keep elbows and arms off of the table.*

7. Refrain from boisterous talking and laughing.

8. Never laugh at an accident or misfortune at the table.

9. Do not play with articles on the table. That is bad form.

10. Eat slowly and noiselessly; don't "feed."

11. Avoid talking with food in the mouth.

12. Keep lips closed while chewing and make as little noise as possible.

13. Let your napkin lie, partly folded, across your lap while eating.

14. Do not drink from a cup or glass containing a spoon. When not using the spoon for stirring, let it lie on the saucer or coaster.

15. Never drink from a saucer, and do not drink noisily from cup, glass or spoon.

16. Use the knives, forks, and spoons in the order placed. When in doubt, observe the hostess.

17. Hold your knife in your right hand, not as though it were a penholder, but so that you may easily press down on the back of the knife with the forefinger.

18. Do not use the knife for conveying food to the mouth.

19. Use a fork when eating vegetables and salad. If cutting the leaves of a salad is necessary, cut with the fork.

20. All food should be put into the mouth with the right hand.**

21. Never let the knife or fork hang from the side of the plate to the table.

* This is a safe rule for children, but may be altered by adults who know how to relax gracefully during the meal.
** English people use either hand.

22. At the conclusion of the meal, place the knife and fork across the back of the plate parallel to each other.

23. Eat a little less of everything than you might. Shrink from the slightest appearance of greediness.

24. When the hostess rises, young men, rise and draw back the chair of the girl or woman next to you as she rises and precedes you from the room.

The young person who is so well acquainted with these rules as to make them an automatic part of himself will not be wholly unable to cope satisfactorily with any problem that might confront him at the table. A complete mastery of them gives one sufficient self-assurance to maintain a poise of action for lending grace to his eating.

*   *   *

QUESTIONS

1. Should the salad be eaten with the main course or afterwards?

   Ans. The salad may be eaten with the main course or afterwards, according to the plan of the hostess. She will show by her service or "lead" when it should be eaten.

2. How should pickles be eaten?

   Ans. Pickles should be eaten with the fork from the plate.

3. Should a paper napkin be used the same as a cloth napkin?

   Ans. No, not exactly. The napkin should be opened with great care being exercised to keep it on the lap throughout the meal. Sticking it in the neck of the blouse or top of the vest is very bad form. When the meal is finished, it should be crushed slightly and placed on the table to be destroyed by the waitress.

4. How should a regular drinking glass be held?

   Ans. The glass should be held near the bottom with the fingers on the outside of the glass, not under it. Never have the little finger sticking out.

5. Is it wrong to tip the gravy bowl?

   Ans. Yes, it is wrong to tip any dish to get the last drop. It gives the appearance that enough has not been provided. Ask the waitress to refill the bowl.

6. How should a slice of bread be eaten?

Ans. Never spread or bite an entire slice of bread. Break off the equivalent of one or two mouthfuls, butter it on the bread and butter plate or in your fingers, never on the palm of the hand, and place a small portion of it into your mouth.

7. Should ice cream be eaten with a fork or spoon?

Ans. Brick ice cream may be eaten with a spoon or a fork. Bulk ice cream is usually eaten with a spoon.

8. Is it permissible to read at the table?

Ans. You should never read anything at the table unless you are alone.*

9. When no butter is served, is it permissible to lay the bread on the table cloth?

Ans. Only hard, crusty rolls are placed on the table cloth, and then great care is used to keep the place at the table from looking too mussed. All other bread is kept on the plate.

10. Should a guest leave his napkin folded after a meal?

Ans. A guest should leave his napkin orderly but unfolded on the table. If, however, he is eating several meals with a family and the others fold their napkins, he should fold his also.

11. What must a hostess say in offering a second service to a guest?

Ans. "May I serve you" to whatever she has to offer, without referring to it as a second serving.

12. How must a water goblet be held?

Ans. By the bowl, not by the top or stem.

13. Should the lettuce on a salad plate be eaten?

Ans. Yes. The idea of leaving the lettuce for "manners" is outdated.

14. Should liquid food be eaten from the point of the spoon or the side?

Ans. The side. And be sure that no noise is made in taking it into the mouth.

15. Where does the honor guest sit at the table?

Ans. At the right of the hostess or host. Where there are several, guests are placed as near to host or hostess as is possible.

16. Should the hostess lead the way to the dining room?

Ans. Yes.

* When there is no one but the family present—perfect freedom in anything with well-bred people is permissible.

17. How should the knife and fork be left on the plate?

    Ans. The knife should be placed on the plate directly in front, blade turned toward you. The fork is in the same position, with tines turned up.

18. How may bones or seeds be removed from the mouth?

    Ans. With the hands.

19. What is canapé?

    Ans. An appetizer served at the beginning of a meal. (See any good cook book for description.)

20. What is demi-tasse?

    Ans. Coffee served in after dinner cups.

21. How should the tines of a fork be held when food is being carried to the mouth?

    Ans. Up.

22. Where must a girl place gloves and purse when dining out?

    Ans. In her lap or adjoining chair if it is not occupied. Never on the table.

23. It is proper to cut meat with a fork?

    Ans. Creamed or minced meats, or meat that can be divided by means of slight pressure. Bacon, when crisp, brittle and dry may be eaten from the fingers, otherwise it should be cut with the fork. A knife| may be used to avoid displaying an effort to cut the meat.

24. Should celery, radishes, pickles, etc., be placed on the regular dinner plate?

    Ans. Relishes, jelly or pickles as a meat accompaniment are placed on the dinner plate. Celery should be taken from the dish with the fingers and put on the side of the plate. Do not put such articles on the bread and butter plate.

25. Is it wrong to take juice from the pickle dish?

    Ans. Since the pickle fork is the only silverware for the serving of such, taking of the juice from the pickle dish would be bad form since one's own spoon should not be used.

26. What is the proper manner of eating a baked potato?

    Ans. Break the potato with the fingers, season it without removing it from the skin. Eat with a fork from the skin rather than remove it and mix it on the plate.

27. Should gravy be served by one individual or should it be passed?

    Ans. At the family table the gravy may be passed or it may be served by the host or friend assisting with the serving. If there are servants the gravy is passed to each individual in turn.

28. Should persons begin eating desserts before other table-mates have finished the regular meal?

Ans. Ordinarily the dessert should not be placed on the table with the main course. One waits until everyone has finished the main meal. It is bad taste to eat the dessert when one first sits at the table before the main course. (In institutions, to expedite service, the dessert is sometimes put on at the beginning of the meal.)

29. If a guest upsets something at the table, should he apologize or say nothing?

Ans. Guests should not get "fussed" so as to disturb others. A glance of regret or a murmured word, if the hostess is near enough, otherwise let the waitress take care of the rest. If there is no waitress, the hostess should relieve the situation saying, perhaps, "Don't be disturbed, I have done that so often." If it happens to be water, one may use the napkin to keep it from spreading and another will be supplied and the meal will be continued.

30. Should the host serve the hostess first?

Ans. The hostess is served first and the person to her right, next and proceeding in that direction. If there is maid service, the guests should always be served first. It is customary to serve the hostess if she is not serving so that when others are served, she can begin the meal. (Note: Authors disagree on this, therefore the hostess may arrange as it pleases her.)

31. At a buffet party must the gentleman serve his partner?

Ans. Yes.

CHAPTER III

TABLE SERVICE

*Be wisely frugal in thy preparation, and freely cheerful
in thy entertainment.*—QUARLES.

AT THE TEAS

Being recognized as an ideal hostess is every woman's
desire, and one can attain this by study and practice. Here
are some suggestions to that end.

1. Appear calm and gracious when your guests arrive.
2. Be rested and fresh in personal appearance.
3. Be free to entertain your guest without having to excuse yourself frequently to prepare refreshments.
4. Be ready at all times for an unexpected guest at your
table.
5. Serve delicious yet inexpensive food.
6. A delightful and inexpensive way to entertain is at
afternoon teas. There is the large formal tea, at which
the out-of-town friend may be introduced to your own
circle or small informal tea, for "visiting" among
friends and neighbors.
7. Spread a tea cloth or a lace cloth on a table.
8. Set a large tray with the tea service (tea kettle, pitcher
and lemon dish, teapot, sugar bowl, tea cups, saucers,
spoons, tea plates piled with napkins) near. On the
other end beyond the tray, set a plate of hot biscuits, or
toast, sandwiches, cookies or cake.
9. Pour tea, adding hot water for those who like it weak,
and putting in sugar and cream or lemon, according
to each one's taste. After the guest receives the cup,
she helps herself to sandwiches and cake.

Use the prettiest tablecloth you have for the dining table.

1. Arrange the decoration,
   a. The centerpiece is usually of flowers.
   b. Use candle sticks.
   c. Place the tea service with cups, saucers, and spoons at one end of the table. The coffee service is put at the opposite end, together with cups, saucers and spoons.
   d. Place dishes of sandwiches and cakes on the table. Put on piles of tea plates and napkins.
2. Serving
   a. The hostess asks (in advance at the day of the tea) two friends who know many of the guests to pour the tea. Their greetings to each guest, as she comes to them to be served, add to her feeling of being welcome, since the hostess herself must remain in the living room to receive her other guests.
   b. Guests help themselves to sandwiches and cakes, candy and nuts from the dishes on the table and sideboard, and stand or sit in groups.

Informal Tea Menu

Chopped Olive Sandwiches

Creamed cheese and chopped nuts with brown bread

Decorated cookies   Assorted pastries

Bonbons   Salted Nuts

Hot Tea

Formal Tea Menu

Assorted Canapés

Sandwiches   Frosted Cakes

Salted Nuts   Bonbons   Mints

Tea and Coffee
Fruit Punch

Lemon   Fruit drops

AT THE BUFFET MEAL

When a hostess must entertain a number of guests, a meal served buffet style is the solution. This form of service, if properly planned, can be most hospitable and enjoyable. Whether in a country home or a city apartment, at morning, noon or evening, the method of setting the table and serving is the same.

In this form of service, most of the food is served from the dining table, serving table and buffet. The guests serve themselves to the food; a part may be served by friends of the hostess or by a waitress. After the guests serve themselves they are seated in congenial groups.

Lay the linen and place the flowers or other decorations in position. Food, silver, china, etc., for the first course are on the dining table when guests are invited to the dining room. Food, silver, etc. for the second course are on the buffet. If there is no maid, the hostess invites some friends to assist, who will pour the coffee while she serves the hot dish. Guests serve themselves from the trays or platters of food on the table and get silver, a napkin and beverage.

For the second course the hostess clears the table and arranges the service for the dessert. Used dishes are removed by hostess or friends. Guests are invited to serve themselves to dessert.

A suitable menu for a buffet meal should be chosen to add to the color scheme of the table. For the main course a moderate menu may be selected. The dessert course may consist of frozen desserts, gelatin dishes, puddings, short cakes and pastries. The beverage may be served with the dessert or with the main course.

In preparation for a buffet table one should try to make it a charming picture of color and harmony.   Doilies or runners, as well as luncheon cloths, are suitable.

Serving forks and spoons, when used alone, are placed at the right of the serving dish.   Silver for individual use will depend upon the number to be served and the amount and character of the foods served.   Silver may be placed on one side of the table so that the guests may get it after serving themselves.

Plates are stacked at the left of the serving dish.   Napkins, usually small, are placed in an orderly arrangement.

Salted nuts may be placed in suitable dishes on the buffet, or the serving table.

SUGGESTED MENUS

Buffet Luncheon

Stuffed Tomatoes in Aspic (Lettuce bed)
Celery Hearts   Cheese Biscuits
Cheese and Jelly Sandwiches
Chocolate Cake
Salted Nuts   Mints
Tea or Coffee

Buffet Supper

I

Stuffed Eggs in Gelatin
Tiny Baking Powder Biscuits
Ice Cream and Cake
Coffee

II

Frozen Fruit Salad
Rolls   Stuffed Celery
Hot Chocolate

III

Cold Cuts with Aspic
Rolls   Butter
Chocolate Cream Pie
Coffee
(Summer)
Iced Grape Fruit Juice
Stuffed Tomatoes
Ripe Olives   Muffins
Ice Cream   Nut Cookies
Coffee

DINNER SERVICE

TABLE SETTING

The appearance of the dining table has a psychological effect on our appetites, therefore it should be as attractive as possible—correctly set, and everything on it spotlessly clean.

After the table has been laid neatly, the next step is the arranging of those articles required by the meal.

The forks are put, prongs up, to the left of the plate or place, in the order in which they will be used. The one farthest from the plate is used first, and the one nearest is used last. At the right of the place go the knives, each cutting edge toward the plate; spoons right side up, their order starting from the outside. To the right and above the forks is the butter plate. The butter knife is laid across it. (Butter plates used at luncheon, breakfast and supper.) At the right, above the knives, is the water tumbler. If other beverages are used the glasses are arranged in a straight line that slants toward the edge of the table.

The table napkin, folded in half or left in a small square, is put at the left of the fork. The individual salad plates are put at the left of each plate. Salt and pepper containers are placed in the center.

The carving knife and fork are placed at the right of the meat platter, the fork nearest the platter. At the right of each vegetable dish a large spoon and fork are placed.

Foods bought in jars and bottles must be removed from them before they are served.

A centerpiece of flowers or fruit always improves the appearance of a table.

USE OF TABLEWARE

Don't hold your eating implements as if they were shovels. When cutting meat don't allow your fingers to touch the blade or fork tines, and don't let your elbows protrude. Cut only one piece of meat at a time. Never cut anything with your knife that you can cut with your fork. Don't overload your fork, or put several foods on the fork at one time. Knife and fingers should never be used as pushers. Use a piece of bread for this purpose.

To serve yourself with two implements, the spoon held in the right hand, is slipped under the portion. The fork is held in the left hand and used to hold the portion on the spoon.

When the knife is not in use, it should be placed on the outer rim of the plate, cutting edge toward you. Hold the prongs of the fork up when eating vegetables; don't spear them.

When you have finished eating, or your plate is to be passed for a second helping, place the end of the knife in the center of the plate with cutting edge toward you, the fork nearest you.

When you have finished eating, do not push your plate away from you or stack dishes.

If it be necessary to leave the table, be sure to excuse yourself first. When a woman must leave the table, and when she returns, the man at the left helps with her chair, the other men rise half-way from their seats.

At a family dinner the ladies of the household follow the eldest and the men are the last ones to enter. The oldest female sits first, the men follow after helping with the chairs.

When there are guests present, the hostess stands by her own chair and tells each where he or she should sit, the lady of honor at the host's right, the gentleman of honor at her right. All remain standing until she makes a move to sit down, her chair being drawn out by the gentleman at her left.

At a formal dinner the host invariably sits at the head, to which he advances at once with the woman guest of honor, and the hostess sits at the foot.

Husbands and wives should never be seated together, neither should brothers and sisters or near relatives.

Members of the entertainer's family should not, unless in exceptional cases, where the dinner is given in their honor, be given the seats at either right or left of the hosts.

The guest of honor or company, seated at the right of the head of the house, is served first. Then the other guests are served in order of their seating, without distinction as to sex.

Once you are seated, sit easily and erect, and keep your feet in front of you on the floor. When you are eating, don't lean back in your seat, on the table, or bend down to your food.

Chapter IV

AT SCHOOL

*How empty learning, how vain is art, but as it mends
the life and guides the heart.*—YOUNG.

Every school has a certain definite set of regulations
which its students are required to follow in order to maintain discipline and assure the smooth-running of the sched-
ule. Persons with varying degrees of power are charged
with seeing that the regulations are kept. Aside from this,
however, there is a standard decorum that the student himself should foster in order to express himself to the best
advantage, and exhibit the right attitude toward the other
fellow. The cultivation of traits of honor, thoughtfulness,
politeness, honesty, order and proper appreciation of values
is just as much a part of education as is the storing up in
one's mind of a vast accumulation of historic, mathematical
and scientific facts.

THE CLASSROOM

1. Always greet the teacher when meeting for the first
time, whether it be morning or not.
2. Be sure that you have everything you need—text,
paper, pen, etc. Don't be a carpenter without tools.
3. When called on to recite, always make some sort of
reply. Don't sit dumbly in the seat and say nothing.
Don't even *think* too long. Valuable minutes are
wasted thus.
4. When standing or sitting, hold yourself erect. Don't
slouch. Talk clearly and sufficiently loud for everyone
in the room to hear.

5. Don't make a habit of laughing at the mistakes of others. This often hinders a person from doing his best.

6. *Don't deface property.* Writing on or cutting into desks and chairs, writing and drawing in books, breaking the backs or turning down the corners of pages of texts are evidences of poor training.

7. Make it *your* business to keep the room in order. Straighten the shades, keep the floor and desks free of waste paper and erase the boards when they need it.

8. *Don't cheat.* You will never learn by "copying" from your neighbor or from the book.

9. Do not argue with or contradict the teacher in class. If you think that she has made a mistake, wait until the hour is over and discuss it with her quietly at the desk.

10. Do not yell out the answers to questions; wait until you are called upon. The teacher will let you know when concert recitation is desired.

11. Don't mistake the classroom for a lunchroom or a bedroom.

IN THE CORRIDORS

1. If there are monitors, respect them and obey their orders.

2. Do not run through the halls or up and down the stairways. Walk.

3. Do not congregate in the halls to talk. Standing groups hinder the passage of traffic.

4. Do not be noisy in the halls any more than in the classroom or assembly hall.

5. In passing from one room to the other, keep to the right. This will avoid confusion. Should you run into someone, take time to excuse yourself graciously.

6. If you meet one of your teachers or your principal stop and say, "Good morning, Mr. Green." Don't fling out a short "how do" while you rush on your way.

7. Do not push your way along into and out of doors. Wait your turn. It is much easier and faster.

IN GENERAL ASSEMBLY OR CHAPEL

1. Enter the hall in an orderly fashion, find a seat and keep still. If it is a secular occasion, it is permissible to talk in conversational tones before the program begins. If a chapel service, there should be no talking at all.

2. Keep your mind and your eyes on the person or persons performing. Assume an attentive position. Don't lean on your elbows, drop your head, or slouch in any manner.

3. If someone comes into the room behind you, or otherwise causes a disturbance, do not turn around to see who it is. Let the performer continue to have your attention.

4. Don't repeatedly look at the clock or your watch. That says to the performer, "I wish you would hurry and finish."

5. Do not laugh at mistakes. If something goes wrong, sit quietly until it can be corrected.

6. Don't write in the song book, on the back of seats, etc. Keep your feet off the seats. Your feet belong on the floor.

7. Participate whole-heartedly in whatever group work is done. Sing, read and yell with enthusiasm. Be sure, however, to keep with the others. The effectiveness of group work depends upon the uniformity.

8. Always applaud a performer when such is in order. Have him know that you appreciate either the performance or the effort. Be sure, however, not to overdo it.

9. Always recognize the entrance of a person of importance by standing in a body. Remain standing until the person is seated or acknowledges you in some fashion.*

10. If you come into an exercise late, do so as quietly as possible. Try not to disturb anyone. Do not walk heavily, and sit down as near the door as possible.

ON THE PLATFORM

1. When seated, be sure to keep the knees together and the feet on the floor. If it is more comfortable for you to cross your legs, be sure to cross them at the ankles and not the knee. Be sure also, not to stretch your legs out in front of you. They should be kept close to the chair.

2. When standing, stand erect with the feet not more than three or four inches apart. Do not lounge on the back of a chair, the table or pulpit. Rest your hand or your elbow on it if you so desire, but not in such a way as to have your audience believe you would fall if it were removed.

3. Remember that talking from the platform requires a clearer enunciation and a slower speech than ordinary conversation. Don't rattle off or muffle what you have to say. If your audience can't understand you, you might as well not be talking.

4. If the audience laughs at or applauds something that you say, do not try to continue talking until the noise

* If a class is in progress, students stand only when visitor is introduced.

has subsided. Just hold your position or acknowledge their act by a smile and a slight bow.

5. Above all, try to avoid an appearance of stiffness or uneasiness. Be natural.

6. If you have to walk a long distance across the platform before reaching your seat, do so as noiselessly as possible. Don't put your whole weight on your heels.

The emphasis that has been placed in late years upon the freedom of the student and the abolition of regimentation has in many cases resulted in rudeness and license. Where there is no demand for order and culture there must be desire for the same, else education is a failure.

Chapter V

AT CHURCH

I never weary of great churches. It is my favorite kind of mountain scenery. Mankind was never so happily inspired as when it made a cathedral.—R. L. STEVENSON.

Church-going is rather out of the custom of many people now-a-days. The radio, the movie, the Sunday concert may amuse, entertain, and inspire, but the hour of worship, that lifts man out of his daily routine and exalts him in a sense of guidance, power and protection without, gives a type of inspiration that endures long after the experience is past. So many great souls have found themselves in meditation before an altar consecrated to the highest and best in mankind, the immortal, the one God of the Christian Religion. Whatever religion in any form may lack, the out-going of one's self, the sacrifice of one's desires for noble ends, which in itself is the very kernel of the teachings of Jesus, transcends any joy derived from achievement of material gains.

Church-going should play a major part in the life of every individual, and should be approached in a spirit of respectful reverence. A person does not go to church in the same attitude as to the theatre or to a concert. Consequently he should keep in mind the following things:

1. Arrive at church on time. The opening exercises are as much a part of the service as the sermon.
2. Sit as near the front as you possibly can and yet remain comfortable.
3. Always participate whole-heartedly in the congregational singing, reading or prayer.

4. Bow your head and close your eyes during a prayer or the singing of "Amen" at the end of a hymn.

5. Look at the minister, soloist, choir or whoever is performing during the service. It is difficult to address an audience that appears sleepy or disinterested.

6. Follow the rest of the congregation as it sits, stands or kneels. Do not remain seated while others are standing.

7. Refrain from general conversation and visiting during the taking of the offering.

8. Eliminate talking entirely unless under very pressing circumstances.

9. Do not ever chew gum during a religious service.

10. Always put something in the collection even though your contribution be small.

11. Have envelopes containing money ready to turn in before coming to church. If envelopes are not used, have the correct amount of money so that it will not be necessary to make change.

12. If it is necessary to enter late, do so quietly so as not to disturb those who are already interested in the service.

13. Do not lean over or turn around to see what is happening behind you.

14. Do not pencil-mark or otherwise deface hymn books or other literature.

15. Do not leave the service until the benediction has been pronounced unless absolutely necessary.

Homage to God merits a dignity distinctive from that found elsewhere. The above decorum will help furnish the exterior atmosphere which makes possible an inner revelation. The two combined help man to know and feel the Divine Presence.

CHAPTER VI

AT THE CONCERT, THEATRE
OR MOVIES

There is that in theatrical representation which awakens whatever romance belongs to our character. . . . Our taste for castle-building and visions deepens upon us, and we chew a mental opium which stagnates the other faculties, but wakes that of the ideal.—BULWER.

We go to the movies, the theatre or to any kind of concert or recital in order to enjoy the performance that may be given there. We like to become so absorbed in what we see and hear that we personally experience every heart-throb and perilous encounter of the hero on the screen. Thoroughly transplanted to the life depicted on the stage, we scheme and plot with crafty Shylock to demand our pound of flesh, or we drift mystically along with the strains of Debussy's "Clair de Lune," completely oblivious of the prosaic world around us.

But how easy it is for us to be brought back to reality with a sudden irritating shock by the thoughtlessness of a neighbor observer. In order not to be one of those who unwittingly destroy a pleasant evening for someone else, follow these suggestions. Some of them apply to practically any type of public performance. Others hold true only under specific circumstances.

GENERAL

1. If there is no usher, the boy precedes the girl down the aisle, finds seats for both of them, and then steps back while the girl enters the seat first. If there is an usher,

the girl precedes the man—both of them following the usher.

2. If the girl wears a large hat, she should remove it so as not to obstruct the view of persons sitting behind her.

3. Refrain from making audible comments concerning the performance or from engaging in loud, sustained laughter.

4. Sit still in your seat. Constant moving about disturbs others.

5. Do not monopolize the arm of the seat. It is to be used by persons on either side of it.

6. Be sure that you know when to laugh. DO NOT MISTAKE TRAGEDY FOR COMEDY.

AT THE MOVIES

1. If there is no usher to direct you, stand in the back of the house a minute or so until your eyes become adjusted to the darkness. This will avoid stumbling over other persons in an effort to locate a seat.

2. When going into or leaving a seat, do so as quickly as possible so as not to long interrupt the story for the others. Try to leave or enter when there is a "break" in the showing.

3. If eating is permitted, make the least possible noise with paper wrappings and peanut shells.

4. Do not use the theatre for petting. Public petting is always bad taste.

5. If the theatre is crowded, do not wait to see the picture through twice. Leave and make room for others.

AT THE CONCERT OR PLAY

1. Be sure to arrive and be seated before the lights are dimmed.

2. Check the number of your ticket with the number of your seat. This will avoid any possibility of having to move later.

3. At a musical, applaud after every group of songs, not after each selection, unless the separate performance is unusually fine.

4. If there is an intermission, when the audience leaves the hall, be sure to be in your seat before the lights are dimmed for the second half of the performance.

This is a theatre-going age. Consciously and unconsciously we mold our characters and model our lives after what we see and hear. The actors do their part from the screen and stage. Let us, in the audience, remember that we too must bear our share of the responsibility of making an enjoyable performance.

* * *

QUESTIONS

1. If three couples go to a recital, to the show, etc., is it correct for each gentleman to sit next to his company?

   Ans. It is good form, but where there is a general acquaintance and general friendliness, men may exchange places with each other.

2. Should a young lady hold a young man's hat in her lap at the movies?

   Ans. No. It is not good taste. A young lady does not take a young man's hat or stick unless he is an invalid.

3. Should a young lady thank her escort for a lovely evening immediately after leaving the place or after he has taken her home?

   Ans. After he has taken her home. She assures him that she has had a nice time and then goes into the house. She may comment on the pleasant evening in her conversation on the way home.

CHAPTER VII

AT THE DANCE

Where wildness and disorder are visible in the dance, there Satan, death, and all kinds of mischief are likewise on the floor.—GOTTHOLD.

Much of the grace and beauty that once placed dancing on a high artistic plane has been practically discarded as this form of entertainment has become more and more universal. True as this may be, no one can help, even now, admiring the young lady who demeans herself on the ballroom floor as though she were dancing the minuet, or the young man who guides his partner across the floor with all the gentility of a Chesterfield. Rhythmic steps come and go, dance hall courtliness rises and wanes, but the ART of dancing moves the even tenor of its gracious way, unperturbed, and the amateur delights in the social courtesies that help maintain this artistic standard. Awkwardness, indecision, and self-consciousness have no place here where beauty, grace and charm should reign supreme. If every dancer will keep in mind the following things, social dancing may still be placed among the arts.

1. A girl should always be ready when her escort arrives.
2. If there are wraps, the boy should take the girl's and his own to be checked while the girl waits nearby for him to escort her into the hall.
3. The boy should take the first and last dance as well as the first dance after intermission with the girl he has brought to the dance.

4. In asking for a dance, the boy says, "May I have this dance?" The girl replies, "Yes, you may," or "I am sorry, but this dance is taken."

5. A girl may refuse to dance, but she should not refuse one boy's invitation and then accept that of another for the same dance unless it was previously engaged.

6. The girl should not entwine her arms around the neck of her partner. Her left hand should rest gracefully on his right shoulder and her right hand be held loosely in his left hand with the arm extended. The boy's right hand should be carried under the girl's left arm and placed just below her shoulder blade.

7. The girl should not lean her head against her partner's shoulder or cheek. She should hold her head erect—slightly to the side if she desires.

8. Excessive movements of the body are very ungraceful. Remember that dancing should be done with the feet, not the torso.

9. Petting on the dance floor is very much out of order.

10. Fancy steps are bad taste at a public dance unless the greater portion of the dancing is of that type.

11. It is bad form for a boy to "cut-in" on a dance unless the dance is designated as such.

12. If in dancing one couple bumps into another, the boy apologizes. The girls says nothing.

13. Loud talking, boisterous laughing and chewing gum are to be strictly avoided.

14. All dancers should refrain from anything suggestive of the obscene.

15. Dancers should move freely around the floor in a counter-clockwise direction. Slow dancing on one spot is to be avoided.

16. A boy should not leave a girl in the middle of the dance floor. He should ask her where she wishes to

be seated, escort her to that place, thank her for the dance and withdraw.

17. A girl should not walk frequently across the ballroom floor alone.

18. A boy should not sit during a dance while there are girls whom he knows that are not dancing.

19. Girls should not dance with strangers except in a very select group.

20. If a boy is introduced to a girl, it is discourteous for him not to ask her to dance unless he is engaged for the immediate dance.

21. If a girl must go home before the dance is over, her escort should take her. They should be sure to excuse themselves to the hostess.

22. A boy should always ask for a dance with the hostess.

23. When leaving, the boy and girl say goodnight to the hostess and thank her for a pleasant evening. They may say, "Goodnight, Mrs. X, thank you. It was a delightful party."

24. A boy should take a girl directly home after a dance and not stop for eating, etc. At the door he bids her goodnight and leaves. He should not go into the house.

Dancing has been so generally adopted that everyone should make it a point of knowing and observing its proprieties. There are advantages attached thereto which do not limit themselves to the ballroom. Chesterfield said, "Learn to dance, not so much for the sake of dancing as for coming into a room and presenting yourself genteelly and gracefully. Women . . . cannot forgive a vulgar and awkward air and gestures." The desire should always be to make of the ballroom "a great market place of beauty."

QUESTIONS

1. How should a young lady refuse a dance?

    Ans. The young lady should always thank the young man in some such manner as this: "Thank you, but may I be excused for this dance?" She should never give the impression that she does not want to dance with the young man at all.

2. If the young man asks one of two ladies who are sitting together for a dance and she refuses, is he supposed to ask the other lady?

    Ans. There is no reason why he should. He should merely excuse himself and go on. The second young lady should not even expect to be asked, but if she is, it is not bad taste for her to accept.

3. After a dance is over, should the young lady link her arm in the young man's or should the young man take her arm?

    Ans. At formal dinners and dances the gentleman offers his arm to his partner.

4. Is it correct for a young girl to applaud after each dance if she wants to show that she enjoyed it?

    Ans. The young lady should never applaud to show her appreciation for a dance. That is the privilege of the young man. If, however, the applause is for the orchestra, both the young lady and the young man should applaud.

5. If a young lady is dancing and wants to stop, is it her privilege to stop?

    Ans. It is the privilege of the young lady to stop, but she should do so only if it is absolutely necessary. Then she may say to her partner, "May we sit out the rest of this dance? I feel a bit tired."

6. What is the proper way for a gentleman to ask a lady for a dance?

    Ans. If the gentleman is speaking to the lady whom he has escorted, it is quite proper for him to say, "Shall we dance?" But if he is speaking to any other young lady, he should say, "Will you dance with me?" or "May I have this dance?"

7. Should a girl walk across a ballroom floor alone?

    Ans. "In other days a girl never crossed the floor alone. In this free age she may go where she will at private or public dance. So it behooves her to acquire an easy, graceful carriage. She must never stride or slide."

8. If a lady asks to be left alone after a dance has been finished, should the young man insist on returning her to the place where he found her?

Ans. No. She may be taken to a place of her choice. "At the close of the dance, the boy asks the girl where she wishes to be seated."

9. When may a young man ask to sit out a dance?

Ans. The young man asks to sit out a dance only after he has danced with the young lady, unless she is his special company.

10. If a girl refuses to dance with one man may she accept another immediately?

Ans. No.

11. May a girl say, "I enjoyed the dance" or "I thank you"?

Ans. A girl should never thank a boy for a dance, but she may say "I enjoyed the dance."

12. Is cutting in at a dance ever approved by good etiquette?

Ans. Yes. Now-a-days at school dances, and at dances where it is understood that people know each other, boys may cut in. This means that the gentleman slightly taps the other gentleman on the shoulder and he relinquishes his partner to the other person. Consider it bad taste where there is no understanding that such will be the form of dancing.

13. If a girl introduces a man to a party of friends, must he ask one of them to take the next dance with him?

Ans. Unless the young man is already engaged to dance with someone else, he should ask one of the party to whom he has been introduced to dance.

14. What is the most courteous way for a man to make a request of a young woman for a dance or for supper at a party?

Ans. "May I have this dance with you?" "Will you take the next dance with me?" "May I have the pleasure of taking you in to supper?"

15. Must a man be introduced before asking a girl to dance with him?

Ans. A man should be introduced before asking a girl to dance with him. At informal school parties where young men bring in their friends, understood to be of equal standing, the young man may take the liberty to introduce himself to the girls in the group by saying, "I am Mr. Hummons, may I have the pleasure of dancing with you?" After the dance has started the young woman may also introduce herself by calling her name, "Miss Ricks" or "Elaine Graham." The young woman should not, however, take too many dances with this young man until she has had a chance to find out more about him.

Chapter VIII

DRESS FOR GIRLS

The body is the shell of the soul, and dress the husk of that shell; but the husk often tells what the kernel is.—Anonymous.

To be able to dress well and appropriately is a satisfaction beyond measure to any one of feminine form. To be able to go and come and mingle at ease with one's friends and forget all about it, so to speak, is the height of attainment in proper grooming.

Two very important things must be taken into consideration. What can I wear that will make me most attractive? To what occasions shall I wear this or that?

The high-school girl has, for the most part, accepted the dress of sensible college girls, and no longer dons frills and laces for school. Sweaters and skirts, pretty washable tailored prints, suits, sensible shoes where standing or walking may be made comfortable are always in good taste.

A girl must study herself and, regardless of the style, buy the thing which is most becoming to her. Clothes properly chosen, even few in number, add personality and poise to the wearer.

It is possible for a girl now-a-days to find, in the various little shops, exact copies of expensive models. Artificial silk and rayon manufacturers have made the ordinary buyers into patterns of propriety and elegance that any aristocrat could afford to copy.

The color of one's eyes, the color of one's hair and the complexion must determine the choice of color in clothes, especially in those things that come close to the face.

In addition to the special care that should be exercised in choosing clothes in accordance with her physical characteristics, there are other specific things which every girl should do to afford herself the greatest comfort with correctness. Different occasions make different requirements, and it is just that which is to be now considered.

SCHOOL ATTIRE

1. School clothes should be simple and made of materials that resist dirt, that can be easily cleaned, and can stand hard wear.

2. Do not wear old party or afternoon dresses to school. If you must be economical, and use dresses of that type, fix them over for Sunday or dinner wear. They have no place in the classroom.

3. Wear sensible comfortable shoes with flat or a regular walking heel. High heels of any sort should not be worn to school. It is preferable also to choose a shoe made of hard-finished leather, such as kid or calf skin. This, however, will be regulated by the current styles.

4. Socks are accepted for general wear now in most schools. A girl should be sure, though, that socks become her personality and harmonize with the rest of her attire. They can be worn nicely with sweaters and skirts, print dresses, etc. Don't wear socks just because everyone else is wearing them. They should never be worn to dinner, to a recital or to church services, even if it is on a campus, unless on a very small girl.

5. Don't try to out-dress your schoolmates. Be guided by what the majority wear. Don't be conspicuous in dress. The school should not be a fashion show. Be discreet in your choice of clothes.

6. Do not wear much jewelry. A watch, a simple ring or pin is in good taste, but avoid flashy rings and dang-

ling earrings and necklaces. A string of small beads or a simple gold chain sometimes adds to the neckline of a sweater.

SHOPPING

1. Always wear a practical street dress, never the same thing which you have been wearing around the house or at work.
2. Be sure to have hat, gloves and purse. *Never* go shopping, or be seen anywhere on the street before five o'clock p.m. without a hat. In college towns where the people are largely active for the college the opposite is permissible.
3. A street shoe with walking, Cuban or flat heel should be worn to afford comfort.
4. When buying body clothes which must be tried on, be sure to wear a dress than can be easily removed and put on, one without many buttons, snaps, sashes, etc. Be sure, too, that it is a dress which does not easily wrinkle.

TEA

1. Guests should wear afternoon or street clothes, medium or high-heeled shoes, hat and gloves. For school teas girls may wear afternoon prints or so-called Sunday dresses without hats or gloves.

DINNER

1. Girls should always dress for dinner, whether at home or school. And when there are invited guests, long dresses with sleeves are quite appropriate. If the dinner is formal, sleeveless evening dresses with appropriate slippers may be worn. Decolleté is unnecessary, unless the dinner takes the form of a large affair, followed by a reception, etc.

RECEPTION

1. Receptions vary. They may be simple afternoon or evening affairs or they may be formal. In the case of the latter, formal evening clothes should be worn. If the reception is in a hotel or large hall, appropriate evening hats of modern style may be worn. An evening wrap is preferable to the fur or cloth coat, but if the weather demands, either of these may be worn, never into the reception room, however, but checked to be received at the door or in the lobby when leaving.

DANCE

The dance which frequently follows the dinner will have something to do with what one wears to the dinner.

Avoid being bizarre in dress or make-up. Do not be too conspicuous in an unbecoming hair dress. You will attract attention, but those whom you will attract may mark you as an ill-advised, poorly bred, unartistic creature.

* * *

QUESTIONS

1. Must a girl wear her hat and gloves to a formal tea?
  Ans. Yes.
2. When is a woman called "well dressed"?
  Ans. When she is dressed appropriately for the occasion.
3. At what type of evening recital or concert should formal dress be worn?
  Ans. If a special artist is appearing or if it is a formal concert where the persons participating will be expected to appear in evening dress.
4. Is it proper to go to an evening show without wearing a hat?
  Ans. If one is riding in an automobile a hat is not necessary unless the distance is remote. People who live out of town beyond what might be considered suburbs always wear hats when going into town. People who are at the seashore or at any summer colony where much that is formal is done away with do not wear hats.

5. Should long dresses be worn to a morning occasion?

Ans. Long dresses are worn to morning concerts where artists may be appearing or grand opera may be held.

6. Should a sleeveless dress be worn in the classroom or for travel?

Ans. Sleeveless dresses are out of place in the classroom or for travel. The short sleeve covering the shoulder or elbow is in good taste.

7. Should bathing suits be worn without wraps when walking to and from the beach?

Ans. At the seashore places where the town is removed from the beach men go back and forth in bathing suits. Women usually don shawls or beach habits to cover the bathing suits, when they must go any distance to the beach.

Chapter IX

GROOMING

In civilized society, external advantages make us
more respected.—JOHNSON.

Every young girl wants to appear well. This can be accomplished only by careful attention to details. Whether a girl is served by a maid or works to make her own living, or pays her own way through school, certain established fundamentals in character should govern her attitude toward those habits of industry, such as mending her own clothes, laundering her linens and silks, taking care of her nails and hair.

It is quite the habit now for one to have one's hair dressed at a beauty parlor regularly. But certain definite care during the interval saves time and expense and adds to the general appearance.

The daily habit of setting aside what is going to be worn the next day, choosing the accessories, cleaning and polishing the shoes, pressing out the wrinkles (and these instructions are applicable to boys as well), will facilitate the morning preparation for school or business and assure one of being well attired. A few suggestions might be helpful.

1. Freshness and daintiness have as their foundation cleanliness. A good shower bath is at all times stimulating and refreshing and adds to one's buoyancy of spirit. Some form of bath should always be taken after strenuous exercise. The bath should always be followed by the use of an effective deodorant.

2. Do not substitute alcohol rubs or toilet water swab-
bings for cold or tepid showers. Perfume will not take
the place of good "sudsy" water.

3. Women who wear sleeveless dresses, bathing suits or
socks should be careful to use a depilatory before don-
ning them.

4. The price of dry cleaning is within reach of the average
girl. She must take time and pains to sort her clothes
weekly to detect the slightest body odor which would
require the process of cleaning.

5. Hose should be changed and washed daily. This not
only adds to the cleanliness but also adds to the life of
the hose.

6. Time should be taken to see that seams of stockings
are straight and that they are not wrinkled at the heel
or ankle. It is economical to buy two or three pairs
of hose of the same shade and out of taste to wear hose
with runs or plainly seen mends except around home.

7. Shoes should be kept in repair. Run down heels and
ripped edges do not distinguish students or housewives.

8. With a little inflammable cleaning fluid and a small
piece of cotton one may remove the little stains on
dresses.

9. Be careful of the length of one's slips, and girls who
really care either buy their slips thick enough or pan-
eled so that the dress cannot be "seen through."

10. See to it that the shoulder straps are properly adjusted.

11. The arrangement of one's hair adds to or detracts from
one's general appearance as it increases or decreases
one's power of personality.

Study the contour of your face carefully. What
makes Katherine Hepburn or Greta Garbo or Marian
Anderson *personality plus* may make you *personality
minus.*

The glamour girl may be sweetly attractive against a background painted to bring out her charms, but in ordinary life you cannot always choose your background. So try to paint your portrait so that you will look well in a gilded or plain wooden frame hung on a colorless wall or one adorned with trees and flowers.

12. Except in extreme grooming, wear washable gloves that may be easily kept clean.

13. Better have fewer handkerchiefs well selected, mostly white, with a few to match the prints, than a large number of cheap, gaudy ones.

14. A well-manicured hand, nails clean and polished, well shaped, is a discriminating feature in man or woman. The articles for accomplishing this are few and inexpensive and should be regularly used. A well-cared-for hand has a touch of loveliness.

15. Don't fail to wear some sort of foundation garment if there is even the slightest need. It helps to produce a neat and trim appearance.

16. The wise lady is very careful of her make-up. Lipstick and rouge should give one a natural, life-like appearance, and be used so that they can scarcely be detected.

The fastidious girl follows closely the above advice for she realizes that it is these small details that make or mar her attractive appearance.

Chapter X

TRAVEL

There is nothing that a man can less afford to leave at home than his conscience or his good habits; for it is not to be denied that travel is, in its immediate circumstances, unfavorable to habits of self-discipline, regulation of thought, sobriety of conduct, and dignity of character.—PACKER.

Travel has become a necessity. It has long since ceased to be merely an amusement or a means of satisfying the whims of the curious. In addition to the ordinary transportation from one place to another, it offers a source of learning and appreciating, of improving the mind and satisfying the soul. It offers an opportunity for added knowledge and increased appreciation of nature's varied expression in mountain, valley, river, sea, tree and shrubbery. It offers a chance for comparison in points of beauty in landscape and architecture, and the valuable information gained through observations and contact is practically indispensable in our present society.

In proportion as travel has become more wide-spread, so has there arisen the need for a code of conduct in transit. The more one travels, the more people he meets. The more people he meets the more attention he should pay to the rights and comforts of others as well as take measures to safeguard his own interests. There are bound to arise, frequently, circumstances for which there is no precedent. On such occasions one has only to think quickly and do what he deems best with as little embarrassment to the persons involved as possible. Under ordinary circumstances, however, the following few suggestions will stand a person in good stead.

[83]

BY TRAIN OR BUS

1. Avoid carrying a great many bags with you. If you have more than two large bags, have them checked and placed in the baggage car.

2. Do not carry paper packages unless absolutely necessary. *Never* carry a package wrapped in newspaper.

3. If a porter carries your luggage onto the train and finds you a seat, thank him graciously and give him a tip. Ten or fifteen cents is a good amount unless he does you some special service. In that instance, twenty-five cents is the average for a journey in Pullman services or a day's or overnight journey.

4. If the train is crowded, do not spread your belongings over space that could be occupied by someone else.

5. Avoid loud talking and boisterous laughing. No one is interested in your conversation except the person to whom you are talking.

6. Have your ticket ready to give to the conductor when he calls for it. Don't keep him waiting.

7. Do not chew gum. It is always bad taste to chew gum in public.

8. Do not throw waste paper on the floor or out of the window. The porter will relieve you of this.

9. Do not "force" a conversation with anyone. Be pleasant and agreeable if addressed, but reserved. If strange persons become too familiar or personal in their remarks, answer them in such a way as to remain polite but have them know that you do not care to be further engaged.

10. Do not use the train or public conveyance for grooming which should be done in private quarters. The inconspicuous use of a powder puff or the smoothing of ruffled hair is all right.

BY TAXI

1. Always allow the taxi driver to open and shut the door of the car.
2. As soon as the driver is in his seat, give the address where you wish to go.
3. Do not carry on a conversation with the driver. If he talks to you, answer him but don't insist on conversing.
4. Do not drop trash of any type or cigarette ashes on the floor of the car.
5. When you arrive at your destination, pay the driver after alighting from the car. A tip is not necessary though it may be given. If you have luggage and the driver carries it to the door for you, a tip is in order.

BY PRIVATE CAR—LONG TRIP

1. If you have been invited to make a trip in someone's car, offer to share the expenses. If the host refuses your offer, do not insist.
2. Do not mar the upholstery with cigarette ashes, grease from food, or by putting your feet in or against the seat.
3. Be considerate of the driver. Do not carry on a conversation or bring up other distractions which would call his attention from the road.
4. Avoid being a "backseat driver." One driver at a time is enough.
5. Do not ride with arms or head out of the window.
6. Do not drop waste material along the highway, especially in an inhabited section. Paper and other trash collected together and thrown out in the woods or a deserted field is all right.

7. If you are traveling at night, do not go to sleep and leave the driver to keep a lonely vigil. Be sure that at least one other person is awake in the car.

8. If you have not shared expenses on the trip, express your appreciation to your host by some sort of appropriate gift when you have returned home.

A trip can be greatly enhanced or marred by the observance or lack of observance of little proprieties. At best travel is tiring, no matter how interesting. Just a little thoughtful care in word and deed will help make for restful relaxation.

CHAPTER XI

THE EARMARKS OF A LADY

Fine manners are a stronger bond than a beautiful face.
The former binds; the latter only attracts.—LAMARTINE.

Practically everything listed here is recorded elsewhere in the book, but this summary in the pamphlet given to students on entrance to school has been found of great value in securing immediate practice of these suggestions. The young girl who wishes to make the wheels of life run smoothly for herself and those with whom she comes in contact remembers that:

A lady,
1. Is polite when entering or leaving a room.
2. Passes behind people.
3. Answers and comes when called by teacher or parent.
4. Graciously answers, "Yes, Miss A," when called or "No, Mrs. B," should the reply require such.
5. Uses "Please," "Thank you," "Excuse me," "Good morning, Miss A," "Good-bye," as part of the daily speech.
6. Keeps hands off of other people. (This means continual fingering or fussing at people's clothes or person.)
7. Does not chew gum in public.
8. Awaits her turn; never bruskly pushes ahead.
9. Closes doors quietly; closes doors that were closed.
10. Obeys the rules of the group.
11. Does not laugh at the mistakes or misfortunes of others.
12. Plays fair and works fair.

13. Does not take things that belong to another.
14. Does not mark tools, walls or furniture.
15. Listens to and follows simple directions.
16. Avoids loud and boisterous laughter and conversation.
17. Is always well-groomed, appropriately dressed, scrupulously clean in body and attire with hair carefully arranged.
18. Does not seek dark and secluded places in which to socialize.
19. Does not make advances for acqaintance of young men or go out of her way to attract their attention.
20. Does not sit in parked cars, on campus or highway, without lights.
21. Stands when superiors enter room and offers seat, remains standing unless person takes seat.
22. Rises when persons leave the room.
23. Uses best table manners always.
24. Accepts courtesy of young men graciously.

Chapter XII

THE WEEK-END

*Let the one you would welcome to your hospitality be one
you can welcome to your respect and esteem, if not to your
personal friendship.*

What a glorious privilege it is to leave home, close the
office or forget the campus for a few days and pass the time
enjoying the hospitality of some friend or acquaintance.
We look upon such occasions as interludes of carefree gaiety
in the long stretch of duty and responsibility which ordinarily constitutes living. Here the many concerns of
home and personal affairs are lifted from our shoulders as
we enjoy the companionship and entertainment of others.
Properly considered, such intercourse brings returns of fellowship in untold measure to both guest and host.

THE HOST

1. Be sure to include in your invitation the length of
time your guest is expected to stay.
2. Advise your guest as to the type of entertainment you
are planning so she will be prepared with clothes and
other necessities for the occasions.
3. As soon as your guest arrives, show her to the room
in which she is to stay so that she may unpack her
things and get settled. Then show her the various
parts of the house to which she is to have access.
4. Have the little conveniences handy—coat and dress
hangers, magazines, books, ash trays, a dish of fruit,
candy or nuts, writing paper, etc.

5. Suggest to your guest a good hour for rising so that she will not get up too soon or too late.

6. If there is a general bathroom, let your guest know at what time in the morning it will be available for her use. This will avoid embarrassing situations.

7. Notify your guest of the time for meals and suggest attire for anything out of the ordinary.

8. Be sure that some type of entertainment is provided. This may be merely quiet games, reading, talking or even resting. Have a definite program in your mind so as to avoid looking for something to do. The program may be changed if the occasion arises.

THE GUEST

1. Be definite about the time of your arrival. Don't catch your hostess unaware.

2. Be sure to have all the personal things necessary—toilet articles, writing paper, etc. Even if the hostess has provided them, it is better to use your own.

3. Be on time for meals or any other affair set at a definite hour.

4. Join wholeheartedly in whatever has been provided for your entertainment. Don't give the impression that you don't want to do it.

5. Keep the room in which you are staying orderly. If there is no maid, make your bed and clean your room at a suitable time in the morning—according to the program of your hostess. After the last night, do not make the bed, but turn back the sheet and covers in an orderly fashion.

6. It is a nice thing to bring your hostess some small gift as a token of appreciation. This may be sent from home after you have returned. Remember to write a note of gratitude soon after a visit.

7. Don't be a general nuisance by asking that things be done for you. Attend to all of your business before leaving home.

8. Have everything you bring with you in good condition, and don't forget to bring everything that you will need.

9. When leaving to go home, check back carefully on your things to be sure you are leaving nothing.

10. Don't monopolize all the time of your hostess. Sit down once in a while, keep still and read. You don't need to be amused every instant.

11. Don't disturb things in the house that appear to be of a private or very personal nature.

12. Do not open doors or explore sections of the house not offered to you by the host or hostess.

13. Take care of the property. Don't wear out the rugs by dancing, run up the electric bill with excessive use of light, soil the upholstery or scar the furniture with the soles of your shoes, fill the draperies, etc., full of tobacco smoke or add to the telephone bill.

The guest should recognize the fact that she owes something to the hostess in helping make the week-end pleasant.

The hostess should see that everything is conveniently arranged for the comfort and enjoyment of the guest. No courtesy or act of thoughtfulness should be omitted. Regardless of how the guest responds to the hospitality or acts in any way, the hostess is still the hostess. Also the guest is the guest and as such should be as considerate, appreciative and as little trouble as possible.

Chapter XIII

BOY AND GIRL RELATIONSHIPS

Let grace and goodness be the principal lodestone of thy affections. For love which hath ends will have an end; whereas that which is founded on true virtue will always continue.
—DRYDEN.

What happy woman doesn't look back to the day of her first date, her first boy friend. Men too, through curls of smoke, dream once again of the little girl in pinafore, the first movie night, that all-day picnic, the canoe. If he got started with the right kind of a girl, it haloed his life.

We are known by the friends we seek and by those who seek us. We should be careful in our selection. There is no more beautiful experience than the boy-girl relationship of pure-minded, wholesome, vivacious youth bubbling over with the desire to have some new thrill, fine sport and companionship of going places and doing things.

The Junior Deb parties nowadays among friends have paved the way for the debutante's having a list of close social acquaintants who are proud to be a part of each party as one of the number becomes of age. There are the older brothers and sisters who are glad to make up the group to usher the newcomers into their already "grown-up society group." Friends, like pearls in a great necklace, cluster around the neck of the woods where increasing joy and fellowship abound.

The Golden Rule is the greatest law governing fine friendship, but there are little courtesies, genuine acts of thoughtfulness that keep the law in action. Here are a few:

1. When a young man wants to date a girl, a school girl in particular, he should do so in time for her to get the consent of her parents if at home, or the house mother if at school.
2. A girl must be considerate, not overbearing or dictatorial. She must give the boy plenty of room to be gracious, chivalrous, but confident in his ability to entertain her in a wholesome manner. Some girls insist upon choosing their own form of entertainment regardless of suggestion.
3. A girl must not do all the talking. It is the nature of man to dominate. Feed his pride by letting him get all the glory for the planning of a swell evening.
4. A boy who is refused a date by a girl more than once ought to accept that as final and not intrude further.

Boys, find some medium of entertainment that does not always require money; table tennis, yard tennis, planned outings where others participate, hikes, mountain climbing or swimming. Go to see the golf game or a good game of baseball. Well, if you must spend money, a good movie is worth it, and if you want to be really smart, take the girl of your choice to one of the teams' big football games, and if you can afford to buy her a chrysanthemum, you'll get a smile that will last until football season rolls around again.

Young man, be on time, and girls, always be prompt. There's nothing to be gained by keeping the young man waiting. Always be sure that the places where you take the girls are beyond question.

Do not break dates for any reason other than illness or business that cannot be postponed.

Girls, do not make promises that will compromise you to keep. When you say "No," mean it and do not be coquetted into saying "Yes." Worth-while men will respect you and young boys will make you the "Ideal Girl." Remember too that it is not necessary to cling to the young man at every step. Polite and courteous young men will assist you gently up to the curb, into the automobile and through the crowded thoroughfares.

Women are again becoming the "clinging-vine" type, produced by frills and furbelow in dress. This is all right, girls, if not overdone. Real gentlemen like to do things for fine women. Give them the opportunity to be gallant and chivalrous and show your full appreciation for every little attention.

* * *

QUESTIONS

1. At what age may a girl have a beau?
   Ans. A girl of 15 may, with guidance, have a beau among those of her equals.
2. At what age may a girl seriously begin to think of marriage?
   Ans. At any time between 18 and 21 years of age.
3. Should a girl ask a boy into her home late in the evening after an engagement?
   Ans. Never.
4. How should a girl greet an escort when he calls at her home for her?
   Ans. It is a gesture of hospitality to shake hands at this time. Some member of the family—preferably the mother—should be present to extend a friendly greeting. When the escort arrives at the home, he should not be kept waiting. The young lady should be ready to leave the house.
5. Should a girl ever ask a boy friend to take her anywhere?
   Ans. She may ask him to escort her. But if it is a pay affair, she may suggest going and leave the rest to him.

CHAPTER XIV

INVITATIONS, ETC.

An invitation to a party is a courtesy which should be properly acknowledged, whether formal or informal.

A formal invitation is printed or engraved to be elegant, while an informal invitation may be given on the telephone. The receiver of such an invitation is sometimes at a disadvantage because he is not given time to consult his or her calendar. To refuse, when in doubt, may cause one to miss a fine evening and a splendid opportunity for social diversion and contact.

Don't make the mistake of trying to be too elegant. It is exceeding bad taste to overdo at any time. Neatness and simplicity are often preferred to showy elegance.

All written invitations should be sent out at least ten days before the event. An emergency like a friend dropping in for a few days enroute elsewhere or an invitation to a theatre party or dinner party, even planned in a hurry, may be written in less time. The telephone is a most convenient substitute for informal invitations and recommended for school boy and girl affairs.

These examples of invitations may aid you.

INFORMAL INVITATIONS
General

Dear Vesta,

I am having a few friends in Easter Monday, March the twenty-fifth, at eight o'clock, and I should be very happy if you would come. Cecie, Lenore, and Jeanette will be here and are very anxious to see you.

Sincerely yours,

Mary Louise Bond

Dear Alex,

Please come to dinner on Sunday, April twenty-first, at seven o'clock. Bring Ghretta, Doris, and Raven with you. Will feel bad if you fail me.

Affectionately,

Agnes Nelson

Dear Jean,

I should be very happy if you, Mrs. Henry, and the Doctor would dine with me on Tuesday next at seven o'clock. I sincerely hope that you will say yes.

Cordially yours,

Florence Carroll

Dear Constance,

We are very anxious that you would dine with us after the tennis game on Saturday at seven o'clock p.m.

Will you be kind enough to extend this invitation to James Hubbard and George Windsor.

Very cordially yours,

Margaret and Charlotte Kennedy

May 7, 1940

Dear Lula,

I am inviting Annie Day, Arona, Yvonne, and Caroline to the house Thursday evening, and I want you to come. Andrade says we may dance in her study. Be sure to be here at 8 o'clock.

Very sincerely yours,

Harveleigh Rivera

Invitation for Tea*

Please drop by Charles William Eliot Hall for tea Sunday evening, March 31, 1940, at 6 o'clock.

* Here a visiting card is used.

Formal

Dr. and Mrs. Charles C. Steward
request the pleasure of
Dr. and Mrs. G. C. Simkins'
company at dinner, Tuesday, February the fifth
at seven-thirty o'clock
at their country home

R. s. v. p.

Miss Elizabeth Ray
requests the pleasure of having
Mae Hamlin
and
Vivian Merrick
at the graduation reception of her class
at Agassiz Hall, Radcliff College
on Tuesday evening, the twelfth of June
from six to nine o'clock

Dr. Miller Whitaker
requests the pleasure of
Mr. and Mrs. Fred Sheffield's
presence at dinner
on Monday, April the first
at eight-fifteen o'clock
Kimball Hall

R. s. v. p.

Mrs. Katie L. Sapp
requests the pleasure of
Mrs. John B. Hall's
company at the Teachers' Club
on Thursday evening, March the fifteenth
from half past seven until nine

Galen Stone Hall
March the first

Acceptance

Dr. and Mrs. Fred Sheffield
thank Dr. Miller Whitaker
for his kind invitation to dinner
on Monday, April the first
at eight-fifteen o'clock at Kimball Hall
and are happy to accept

Mrs. John B. Hall
accepts with pleasure
Mrs. Sapp's kind invitation for
Thursday evening, March the fifteenth
from half past seven until nine

32 Winsor Street
Boston, Mass.

Luncheon Invitation

Dear Ruth,

I am having a luncheon in honor of Mrs. Ed. Merrick and Mrs. Garnet Wilkinson Saturday afternoon, March the thirtieth, at two o'clock. I do hope it will be possible for you to come because I have wanted you to meet each other for so long. Just phone me so that I shall know whether to expect you or not.

Your loving friend,

Flemmie P. Kittrell

Week-end Invitation

Dear Hoyt and Frances,

"Kin" joins me in the invitation to have you spend the week-end with us at the seashore. Kindly wire me your acceptance and time of your arrival.

Sincerely yours,

Louise

Letter of Introduction

My dear Hilda,

Olivia Stead and Thelma Thornton will pass through your little station at Talladega on Tuesday, May fifth. I should be very glad to have you see them and offer any little courtesy that your kindness prompts. They are old friends and former teachers in our school. I am sure they will have great pleasure in knowing you.

Affectionately yours,

Lenora Scott

Letter of Congratulation

My dear Marie,

Listening to you over the radio was most interesting. Your voice is beginning to show greater depth of feeling and tone. I suppose Daddy is very proud of you.

Lovingly yours,

Carol

Acknowledging a Visit

Dear Mayme,

You and your household contributed so much to my enjoyment during the few days I was with you in your beautiful seashore home.

Pardon my lateness in acknowledging your hospitality. Come to visit us at your convenience.

We all send love to Bobby, Edward, Mamie Ella and Doctor.

Very sincerely yours,

Élise

Acceptance

Mrs. B. W. Barnes thanks Mrs. J. A. Cotton for her kind invitation to luncheon on Tuesday, April eight, at one-thirty o'clock at Kimball Hall and is pleased to accept.

Formal Regrets

Dr. and Mrs. John Dewey Hawkins regret their inability to accept the invitation of Mr. and Mrs. Harold Trigg for dinner Tuesday, April 8, at 8 o'clock p.m.

Formal Invitation

Dr. and Mrs. Robert Daniel
Friday, April the Twelfth
Estey Hall
Two to Four o'clock

Note of Sympathy

Dear Mrs. Webb:

Accept my profound sympathy for the painful accident to little Reginald. Here's hoping for him a speedy recovery.

Very truly yours,

C. E. Dean

Congratulations on Receiving a Doctor's Degree

Dear Carol:

It pleased me greatly to note your successful completion of your work in psychology and the announcement of your candidacy for the degree of Doctor of Science.

Maud Brooks Cotten

Informal Invitation to Week-end Guest

Dear Joyce:

Will you, Jule, Missie, Doug, and Elise come to Canary Cottage for this week-end? We have lots of fun in store.

Sincerely yours,

Minerva

Informal Invitation to an Automobile Party

Dear Vivian,

Addie and Elinor are traveling by automobile to New York Saturday and would like to have you and Joe join them. I hope that you can find it convenient to do so. You'll have an enjoyable trip.

Sincerely yours,

M. L. Gullins

CHAPTER XV

INTRODUCTIONS

In life there are meetings which seem like a fate.
—OWEN MEREDITH.

Introductions present a problem to many persons, though there really should not be much difficulty involved. The usual custom is to introduce younger people to older people. This plan would work well. "Mary, I want you to meet my friend Mrs. Jones," or "Mrs. Jones, may I present my friend Mary." It is customary also to present a boy or man to a girl or woman, an unmarried person to a married person; guests at a party, reception or at home are presented to a guest of honor.

For young people generally one would say to one's equal, "Charles, this is Carol. Carol, I want Charles to know you." To older people they would say, "Mr. Smith, I want you to know my school friend Lucy or Dannie." "Mother, I want you to know Miss Lawrence." "Father, this is my Physical Ed teacher, Miss Burwell." The football and baseball pal introductions such as "Give him a paw, John" or "Shake hands with Paul" are out of place in a living room.

The reply is of equal importance. The person receiving the introduction should say with a nod or a smile, "How do you do," making sure to call the name. With older people, acknowledgment of an introduction may be made by just repeating the name with a rising inflection. When it is said to several in a group, "May I present Miss Skinner," the persons to whom the introduction is made may say, "Miss Skinner," with a rising inflection.

Shaking hands, a good old-fashioned friendly custom, must be handled with discretion. The one to whom you are presented must take the initiative. Parents, teachers, people of conspicuous station desiring to make people at ease, offer the hand. Under no circumstances must a proffered hand be ignored. Boys and men, on meeting, show signs of good sportsmanship to offer hands to one another.

Boys always stand for introductions. Girls or women rise only when presented to someone of high station, to an older woman or elderly man. A safe rule is to withhold no respect to older persons. One's common sense comes into play here. Always do the thing, rising or even offering a hand, that adds to the comfort and pleasure of the older person.

There is much hesitation on the part of young people or older people thrown together in what is expected to be a congenial group when each has not been introduced to the other. At a party, whether automobile, town or garden, all are supposedly social equals, and being there demands courtesy on the part of all. A girl or woman is within her cultural right to say to the person near her, "I am Mrs. English." The man or the woman acknowledges the introduction by saying with a smile, "How do you do, Mrs. English, I am Mrs. Riley." A conversation could be pursued with interest without sensitiveness or any indication of aggressiveness on the part of either.

When one meets one or two friends on the street or in a store, it may not be always convenient to be introduced, but if the person met wishes to give the introduction it should be done at once.

Never embarrass a friend who attempts to introduce and —as memory is so treacherous—cannot call both names, just accept the introduction as though you understood. If a name is called and there is no hurry, it is not bad taste to say, "I beg your pardon but I didn't get your name." This is absolutely necessary if you are going to be thrown together immediately.

In business, people do often give letters of introduction, but it appears awkward and sometimes embarrassing to attempt to call on people merely presenting a letter of introduction. A much better way is to have one's friends write ahead and say, "My friend, Norvelle Dismukes, is making her home in your city and I'd like to have you know her." The receiver of the letter could either telephone or call to complete the introduction, making room for the cultivation of a friendship between the new-comer and the at-homer. The new-comer should not hurry to return the call, but should certainly not be too long in stopping for a few moments to see the Woods who gave her such a warm welcome to the city.

When you bring other boys and girls or friends into your home, introduce them to your mother, the presiding hostess of the home, although you may be the temporary hostess. Pick out the other members of the family, "This is my sister. I want her to meet all of you," calling them by name. If you want to add a few words, well and good. "Teddy is captain of the football team"; "Foster is our bugler"; "Elsie is the president of her class"; "Victoria plays the piano beautifully, maybe she'll play for you." Make everyone comfortable and at home.

* * *

QUESTIONS

1. How should one introduce one's self when traveling on train or bus?
   Ans. A young woman should never make advances. A young man, after due consideration, may ask a young woman a purely impersonal question (books, scenery, weather) and if she resents his intrusion, he should desist immediately.

2. What are the proper steps in meeting young ladies? In making an introduction, who is supposed to be introduced first, the man or woman?

Ans. Always present the young man to the young woman. For instance, "Dr. Hancock, I wish to present you to Miss Smith," or "Miss Smith, may I introduce Mr. Jones?" "Miss Smith, Mr. Jones."

In case of a person of prominence, a younger woman or persons of less importance are presented to the gentleman of affairs (rare instances).

3. When is it permissible for a young lady to remain seated when she is introduced?

Ans. Remain seated when introduced to women or to men of equality, except the person be hostess.

4. There are certain circumstances under which one should not introduce. What are they?

Ans. When one does not remember a name and can get out of introducing without embarrassing someone, or in case of social inequalities or when people ask introductions of persons known to be disreputable. In some instances, people are busily engaged or hold high rank and should not be disturbed with introductions.

5. What are some substitutes for "How do you do," when being introduced?

Ans. "I am happy to meet you" or just call the names in accepting with a smile or nod of the head as "Miss Leake," "Miss Sharpe," etc.

6. On being introduced, is it necessary to shake hands? Who offers the hand first?

Ans. Only men shake hands regularly. An older or more important woman may offer her hand to young men or women or to persons of lesser station as a gracious gesture of seeming equality or friendliness. A hand should always be taken when offered.

7. Should an older lady be introduced to the younger or vice-versa?

Ans. The younger woman should be presented to the older except when the younger may be a celebrity. For instance, you would present your mother, although older, to Miss Dorothy Maynor, the celebrated singer.

8. Must a man rise for an introduction?

Ans. Always, except when it is given in a moving vehicle or at theatre and concert.

9. What is the courteous thing to say on leaving one just met?

Ans. "I am happy to have met you," "I appreciate the introduction," "I shall be happy to see you again."

CHAPTER XVI

POISE

It is the man who is cool and collected, who is master of his countenance, his voice, his actions, his gestures, of every part, who can work upon others at his pleasure.—DIDEROT.

Poise is that state of mind and condition that expresses a calm and undisturbed soul. One's reaction to varying situations pleasant or unpleasant, the ability for integration, determines to what degree one has developed poise. People who are able to think—and do so continuously—regardless of untoward circumstances, have developed a poise akin to great power. For instance, there's an automobile accident; it need not be serious, but the boy or girl with poise thinks immediately of the nearest telephone to notify those in authority, at home or school, and locates the nearest garage for immediate adjustment of conditions of the car and renders first aid without fluttering or excitement.

Poise is something that can be developed by any woman. A silent pause before entering a reception room, getting a full deep breath before approaching the hostess or attempting a conversation, taking a little time for imaginary conversation, going through the process of introduction before meeting people, being sure that one is comfortably and appropriately dressed for an occasion are some of the surest steps to poise.

SPEECH

The tones of human voices are mightier than strings
or brass to move the soul.—KLOPSTOCK.

To be able to speak well, to enunciate clearly, to pronounce words correctly, to talk interestingly of the subjects of the day, giving evidence of one well read without affectation is an accomplishment to be desired beyond beauty and physical charm.

There enters into this, however, the voice which is the greatest charm of personality. A deep, clear, resonant voice is a priceless gift to any individual, the owner of which will attract however lacking she may be in physical beauty. People who have high-pitched, rasping voices, through certain vocal exercises like taking deep breaths and expelling it through the mouth, resounding out the vowels like a, e, i, o, u, striving for modulation, will, in time, coupled with persistent effort, change the quality of their voices.

A voice that is coarse, low and penetrating jars upon the sensibility of the listener, and oft-times marks a person whose intentions are fine and whose morals are above reproach as an undesirable.

Who does not like to listen over the radio, from the public platform, or in the living room to a well-modulated voice, rich in feeling, well controlled, yet with an enthusiasm that makes the listeners a part of all that's said!

Young people will get rich returns if they will cultivate good speaking voices. It is an asset in business as much as in pleasure.

CONVERSATION

For good or ill, your conversation is your advertisement. Every time you open your mouth you let men look into your mind.
—BRUCE BARTON.

Conversation should be a pleasant and cheerful exchange of ideas. It so often becomes one-sided because the more gifted monopolize the time and attention. The latter indulged in by people otherwise charming and interesting is nevertheless rude and selfish.

One should always choose a conversation that is interesting to the group, not for the purpose of displaying one's knowledge or attracting attention to one's self. Here again the spirit of comraderie ought to be paramount.

That individual who enters a room and gets everybody talking and asking questions and enjoying a conversation where anyone can participate without assuming to dictate or direct the trend of thought is not only truly gifted but frequently sought and welcomed in any group. The shortest way to popularity is through the ability to arouse what is fine and beautiful in the other fellow through giving him a chance to share in the discussion of subjects of common interest. This is true even among the highest of the intelligentsia where available scientific data may be the subject of conversation.

People who are shy and timid, however pleasing their personality, must give a great deal of time and practice to imaginary conversations until they can speak with assurance on subjects in which they are interested. Real speaking power is to be desired by anyone.

SOME THINGS TO BE AVOIDED

1. Do not talk constantly about one's self unless one has been invited to entertain the group with some of his personal life and affairs.
2. Do not protrude the little intimacies of the children of one's family.
3. Try never to say cruel or sarcastic things.
4. Don't be a kill-joy. Use tact. The slightest reference to some unpleasant situation may spoil the whole evening for several persons. Remember that what to you may be a casual remark for you to soon forget, will linger long in the mind of your listeners according to the effects it has upon them and will place you as a person to be avoided or desired.

"Manners make the man, conversation reveals him."

CHAPTER XVII

AT THE TELEPHONE

To a nice ear the quality of a voice is singularly affecting.—TUCKERMAN.

Because it is not possible to look into the eyes of the listener, some persons seem to feel that courtesy is unnecessary in a telephone conversation. Because they see a cold, lifeless instrument directly in front of them, they forget that a living human being is at the other end of the wire. And so there often result abrupt, coarse telephone conversations that fail miserably in what should be their purpose. Here are a few things to be remembered when using a telephone.

1. Do not shout into the mouthpiece. It is not necessary to talk loud to be heard. Well-modulated tones and clear enunciation mean much more.

2. Do not stand very close to or very far away from the mouthpiece. Both positions make it equally difficult to be heard. The mouth about two inches from the phone is a good distance.

3. Show the same politeness to "Central" that you should exhibit to everyone. Do not fail to say "Please" and "I thank you."

4. Do not become impatient and rude if "Central" makes a mistake. Remember that everyone is subject to error.

5. Do not use the telephone for extended visiting. It may cause inconvenience to someone else.

6. The person making the call is the one to end it. It is impolite for the person called to terminate the conversation unless it is absolutely necessary.

It is to be remembered that the business call differs from the friendly call in form as well as in purpose. Brevity and definiteness should characterize the business call, for its object is to convey a message with little expenditure of time. Each time someone speaks he should give as much information as possible. The following is an example. The telephone rings and is answered by Mr. Edmonds.

Mr. E: (Lifting the receiver and speaking into the mouthpiece) "Palmer Memorial Institute, the Office, Mr. Edmonds speaking."

Mr. G: "This is Mr. Grant at the Recreation Center, Greensboro. I should like to speak to Mr. Riley, please."

Mr. E: "Mr. Riley is away from the campus and will not return until tomorrow. May I take a message for him?"

Mr. G: "No, thank you, I must speak directly to him. Please have him call me at 3370 as soon as he returns tomorrow."

Mr. E: "Yes, I shall."

Mr. G: "Thank you."

Mr. E: "You are welcome."

The friendly call made on a private line varies according to the persons and the purpose of the call. Each party in the conversation, however, should let the other know *immediately* to whom he is speaking.

The telephone rings.

Miss McIver: (Picking up telephone) "Miss McIver speaking."

Mr. Lanier: "Good morning, Miss McIver. This is Henry Lanier. How are you this morning, etc."

The call should not be lengthy unless you are positive that it inconveniences no one. Probably a third party is trying to get a message through. It may be that even the person to whom you are talking wants to get back to the dinner table or to friends who have dropped in for a visit. Particularly is it necessary to be careful on a party line. Remember, too, that it is the person who begins the conversation who should, under ordinary circumstances, end it.

In a telephone conversation, the voice means everything. Be sure that yours shows you in your best light.

Chapter XVIII

FOR THE MEN AND BOYS
WHO CARE

The taste of beauty, and the relish of what is decent, just and amiable, perfect the character of the gentleman. . . .
—SHAFTESBURY.

While many of the things written heretofore are applicable to both boys and girls, it seems apropos to include these few pages introducing correct habits for boys and men. A courteous, gallant young man nowadays is a prize to be won by any admiring girl.

Strange it is that people, who under most conditions are considered wise and intelligent, make all kinds of plans for the proper training of their girls and so nonchalantly express their attitude in these words: "Oh, the boys will get along all right."

Give me words, I pray, for that beautiful, sweet girl who knows every move and turn, who becomes suddenly embarrassed on the ballroom floor at the awkward and ungainly demeanor and gyrations of that otherwise bright and active college senior who has been invited as her special escort.

Imagine her anxiety to the point of tears as his right hand guest at the formal dinner when he blows into his soup to cool it, dips it toward him and makes a noise swallowing it. Imagine again her chagrin following him into the seat at the theatre because he wanted to take the seat at the extreme end and didn't know what to do. To avoid these embarrassing situations, we therefore add these pages as an introduction to the personal culture at least expected of men who seek the company of fine women.

[113]

CHAPTER XIX

HOW TO BEHAVE

Behavior is a mirror in which everyone displays his image.—GOETHE.

"Being agreeable" is the highest duty of any human being mingling with other people. Just following a set of rules—being a stilted actor—is far from being well bred. One must be kind and considerate of others, and any rule or art that produces this effect is a part of the fine art of living. Practicing good manners should be as natural as displaying the teeth. Nothing is so painful as to see someone trying to be what he is not. An overpolite man is an affectation to be avoided. A wolf in sheep's clothing has often found his way into a rich fortune. So the crook, in tuxedo or evening coat, has found entré to the heart of an angel in the cloak of etiquette admired by all.

"Manners make the man" is an oft repeated expression. Taken literally, one's first acquaintance may wreck a dozen households before he is discovered. One should know something definite about the man he introduces to his household or friends, either by intimate personal knowledge or confidential correspondence between himself and someone he does know. No one is so poor as not to be friendly with well-known, respectable people or so small, if rightly guided, as not to be seen by those who can advance his interests and help him find his place in congenial human society.

Here then, are a few simple directions for the young man who would desire to be liked, to be sought, to be appreciated in respectable company.

1. Next to being agreeable is a natural thoughtfulness for others—to show a generous spirit, oft-times, "you first, my dear Sir."

2. Be a good listener. Use discretion in advancing the newest topics of the day to show your alertness and supply of current information.

3. Better remain silent than lose your temper in argument. "A man convinced against his will is of the same opinion still." The old adage, "agree with thine adversary," may be thin ice, but it bridges many a chasm.

4. A gentleman is never rude. If he can afford servants, his real self can be best judged by his attitude toward his inferiors in position—though they render him service of a menial nature. There are things which would make a man angry—he would speak, he does speak words of wrath—sometimes of venom but never with coarseness. He rises above street speech by the language with which he lashes the villain who would drag the name of his fair lady in the dust, attack the honor of his family or the integrity of his business. Indeed no one encourages the cowardly in any man. His culture asserts itself in the discretion with which he makes his choice when to speak and when to be silent.

5. A gentleman does not wish to accept favors that embarrass. Invitations and courtesies from friends do not embarrass if one is not in a position to return them.

A dinner guest with Mrs. Warren, friend of the family, joining the automobile party with a classmate, spending the week-end in the home of a chum, knows his being unable to return the same favor does not belittle him in the eyes of a friend, for sooner or later some little inexpensive courtesy, some gracious assuming of responsibility about the house or concern for the

welfare of other guests breeds gratitude and appreciation that no mere return party can give.

6. Don't be a grafter. Don't seek friends for what they
have to offer. You may think you are wise and clever
stopping in for the Friday Tea and the Sunday Tea
without being invited, but you will soon wear out your
welcome.

7. "Being popular" is the natural desire of the high-school
and the pride of the college boy. Being thoughtful, a
good listener, a sincere appraiser of the good in others,
taking your turn gracefully, will gain for you respect
and friendship as the "Good Sport," the jolly good fellow, whom everyone admires.

8. Don't go where you are not wanted. You, of course,
cannot be invited to all of the parties in town, or out
of town (though eligibles are overworked serving so
frequently, since the young debutantes outnumber the
boys).

Nowadays, even at small parties, one must sit at
the door and compel identification, for the number of
their own well-bred young men who take this form of
crashing is unbelievable except to those who experience this most distasteful performance often during
the year. Your father may be the friend of the hostess,
or you may know the girl, but if you have not been
included in the list of invitees, have the good sense
and pride to stay away.

If you want to go bad enough to let some friend of
the family know your motives, she or he may handle
it so deftly that the mother may send a late invitation,
making an apology for the omission. In this case she
would forgive your intrusion.

9. Never be ashamed of being courteous. Maybe the
other men and boys don't remove their hats in the

elevators, but you make it your code to remove your hat where ladies are present, as a symbol of superior up-bringing.

A few remarks on business demeanor. This little book is not really for the bachelor. We have kept in mind the growing boy, the college lad and the recent graduate. He may be serving as a bell boy, errand boy or even secretary. Here are a few hints of how to make good. I do a small business in education and I have had need of all of these forms of service and feel that I do know a few of the pitfalls.

1. Don't argue with the employer. He may never have been to college and maybe his pants aren't properly creased, but he is big enough to guide you in making a living, so give him the benefit of the doubt and forge ahead. If he's wrong, he'll eventually see it. If you are wrong and persist in showing him you're right, you'll see the door some day, never to re-enter.

2. Don't use your employer's time to socialize with the girl employees. Wait until lunch time or until the shrill whistle in the town clock tells you that, "Day is dying in the West."

3. Don't shout through the telephone. You'll drive away prospective customers.

4. Be prompt, be courteous, be on time, be upstanding and businesslike, don't slouch or sit down on your time and rest.

5. Here's a bit of sound advice, young men: Don't keep all kinds of hours and expect to sleep on the employer's time.

6. Be wide-awake, alert, ready to run at any bidding. Many a competent office boy has changed the name on

the inside of the office door when the old employer retired or changed vocations.

7. Don't lose your temper. A man without any temper isn't worth a cent, but he can turn his anger to better advantage than letting it loose in somebody else's office or place of business.

In another place in this volume travel has been discussed, but it may not be amiss to here set down a few things young men will do well to remember.

1. A gentleman will not remain seated in the car if a woman stands near. I realize that bus travel has altered this code of ethics, but the offer shows the gentleman in you, and many women, knowing that maybe you have walked for miles, graciously refuse to add to anyone's discomfort and accept their lot.

2. So often men are in a dilemma as to which is really the most courteous thing to do. So many rules of etiquette like "ladies first" seem out-moded, but gentlemen do precede ladies whom they are accompanying, or older ladies to whom they wish to offer the courtesy of a hand when leaving their cars. They do this for two reasons, first to make room for her exit, second to assist her in dismounting.

3. Don't be afraid of being courteous. A young man of my acquaintance found himself compensated to the amount of $10,000 in a will for stepping off a train and carrying the suitcase of a plainly dressed old lady, putting it into the hands of a porter. She immediately employed a detective to get the young man's name at the next stop. Ten years passed before the postman brought to his door the executor's notice.

4. Don't litter the floor with your newspapers and cigarette stubs. Were you to follow such a one, would it add to your enjoyment?

5. If you are fortunate enough to travel by Pullman, try observing these few suggestions.

   a. Don't monopolize the wash room. Do your toilet rapidly and early, and with as little to say as possible unless the porter tells you that you are the only passenger.

   b. Don't leave your bowl unclean. Suppose you were to follow someone who did. Do you swear, young man? I hope not, but the gods would forgive you once.

   c. If you go to the dining car, be at home. Display your best taste. The waiters recognize quickly well-bred gentlemen and give them a gentleman's service.

   d. Tipping may be a nuisance. Travel in Europe, and you'll be glad to give your porter who brushes you and handles your luggage a ten-cent piece, and for your breakfast waiter fifteen or twenty cents will do. Porters do not expect everyone to tip like bankers.

A little gratuity for special service rendered is never out of place when graciously and unbegrudgingly bestowed, even though it may not be expected.

CHAPTER XX

EARMARKS OF A GENTLEMAN

To be a gentleman is to be honest, to be gentle, to be generous, to be brave, to be wise, and possessing all those qualities to exercise them in the most graceful outward manner.
—THACKERAY.

The popular mind needs to be relieved of the idea that a gentleman is an effeminate, spineless male character who is afraid of his shadow. So deeply has this faulty conception become imbedded in the souls of our men that they seek to be as crude and rough as possible in order to be that much more man. A real gentleman avoids both of these extremes. He is neither cave man nor fop. He is possessed of the greatest possible degree of strength in body, mind and character, which he demonstrates in such a way as to move smoothly and amiably among his associates. He is the man who:

1. Maintains and exhibits a genuine respect for women.
   a. He raises his hat when recognized by a lady and keeps it off while talking to her. If he is outside and the weather is bad, the lady will give him permission to return it to his head.
   b. He stands when a lady enters the room provided such action does not disturb whatever is taking place in the room.
   c. He does not smoke in her presence without asking her permission.
   d. He always assists her in and out of a car and up and down staircases.

e. He always offers his assistance in whatever task she may be performing. If the lady refuses his aid, he does not insist.

f. Refrains from making advances to strange ladies except to offer services.

g. Keeps his hands off of her, except when helping her to ascend into or descend from some position.

2. He is careful to call a person's name when addressing him, and to say "Thank you," "If you please," and "I beg your pardon" when they should be used.

3. Avoids making an unnecessary "scene" under any circumstances.

4. When he makes a mistake, admits his fault and seeks to rectify it if possible. He does not fashion alibis to cover his failings.

5. Keeps himself well groomed and appropriately dressed at all times. Even if he is working he keeps as clean and neat as possible. The fireman's clothes don't have to look like the coal.

6. Assumes a respectful and sympathetic attitude toward the opinions, beliefs, short-comings and mistakes of others.

7. Does not use profane language or tell questionable jokes.

8. Does not take undue advantage of a situation or a person.

9. Opens and closes doors noiselessly and leaves them as he found them.

10. Keeps well informed as to things happening about him of general interest.

11. Lets no opportunity whatsoever escape for improving himself.

The above things should be practiced so regularly that they become a part of the man. "Thoughtfulness for others, generosity, modesty and self-respect are the qualities which make a real gentleman . . . as distinguished from the veneered article which commonly goes by that name."*
To be a gentleman is to be the finest type of man.

* Huxley.

Chapter XXI

SUGGESTIONS AS TO DRESS FOR MEN AND BOYS

Men wear full evening dress to formal functions, although the dinner coat or tuxedo has come into common usage for all social affairs held after six o'clock in the evening. Low cut shoes or pumps are used for evening or dinner wear.

For evening weddings, the full evening dress is correct. For mornings, dress coat with gray and black striped trousers.

Men who want to be correct wear to a formal tea cutaway coats, stiff collars, white shirts, black ties and black shoes.

For an afternoon dance, a man may wear a business coat, colored shirt, handkerchiefs and tie to match. In summer, dark coats and light flannel pants are always in good taste.

Sport attire, comfortable shoes, etc. are worn at camps.

A boy's problem of dress is a simple one. A neat well pressed dark suit may be worn on any occasion that is not formal.

Boys must not be careless and slack. Neatness and cleanliness are necessary always and give character and poise.

Sweaters are in good style, for sport or out of doors, but cannot take the place of coats.

Boys should always wear coats to formal school assembly or to dinner.

A boy may be coatless at an outdoor party, but a coat should always be worn indoors except when participating in indoor games or sports.

Sport clothes for dances for school boys are in good taste at informal affairs.

Boys may wear gloves for complete dress.   One is removed when shaking hands.

Boys must never be conspicuous from use of highly scented soap or toilet water.

CHAPTER XXII

IF YOU MUST INDULGE

Let the world have whatever sports and recreations please them best, provided they be followed with discretion.—BURTON.

Smoking is a harmless diversion for those who are old enough to make their decision on all matters of conduct.

For high-school boys and girls who are dependent upon their parents or guardians for support and for making and carrying out of their plans, the tendency to follow their advice in such matters is a sign of good breeding. The youth who gets a satisfaction out of the "smartness," in breaking over school or home regulations in regard to this habit, thinks it is an expression of his or her individuality when after all, it is a mere indication of the lawlessness that will break out later somewhere else with more serious consequences.

While science has not legislated against tobacco as injurious to youth, it has given positive proof of the effects of nicotine on the nervous system.

For those who find, within their rights, satisfaction and pleasure in smoking, here are a few facts it will be well to remember.

1. Girls, do not smoke while walking on the street. This makes you too conspicuous. There are some things a gentleman can do that just don't become a lady.
2. Don't smoke in the coaches on trains. Men don't do this as much as women. There are still many folks who don't smoke and do not care to be annoyed by cigarette fumes.

3. Be sure to always knock the ashes from your cigarette in an ash tray—not on the floor, in the flower vase or in the dishes.

4. If you are a habitual smoker, be sure that you are provided with cigars or cigarettes and some form of light. Don't always borrow.

5. Don't light your pipe or cigarette in a private home unless you know that there is no objection. If you are not sure, ask.

6. Don't smoke in an automobile where there are persons other than yourself unless you have their consent.

7. Boys, don't take for granted that every woman smokes. There are many who do not. Always ask a lady's permission before smoking in her presence.

8. Be careful in handling lighted cigars or cigarettes. Burnt upholstery in automobiles and chairs and, even more serious, damage by fire often results from carelessness in this regard.

Women, in their effort to show how far the ban has been lifted from their smoking, have made the habit much more of a nuisance than it was when it was considered solely a man's prerogative.

The average man takes his smoking as a type of relaxation and a source of comfort. His pipe is as close a friend as his favorite dog. But it is different with the average woman. She smokes in places and under circumstances which the man would consider most improper—all for the sake of exhibiting her independence.

For those who must smoke, both men and women, be sure to make of it a personal consolation and pleasure—not a public nuisance.

QUESTIONS

1. Should a man offer cigarettes to a lady if he does not know whether or not she smokes?

   Ans. Since it is so general among women, it is perfectly natural for one to assume and therefore offer the courtesy.

2. Is it proper for a man to give a lady cigarettes for a gift?

   Ans. In certain society where people feel free to indulge in exchange of sports and gifts in keeping with their tastes, it would not be out of order. Those who adhere to conservative ideals would prefer purchasing their own.

3. If a girl is at a party where smoking is being done generally, is it impolite for her not to smoke?

   Ans. By no means. It is a sign of weakness for a person who has convictions on any particular form of entertainment or action to follow the crowd for fear of them. Here the tables are turned. It is impolite and unkind for anyone to insist on your doing anything contrary to your code of ethics or social behavior where nothing is to be gained by so doing.

4. If a girl goes out with a boy, should she smoke if he doesn't?

   Ans. A truly fine girl, at this particular stage of the habit which assumes a public attitude not wholly accepted, would prefer finding her amusement and satisfaction in refraining from being conspicuous. An example of self-denial here would very likely raise her in the estimation of the young man. No man truly loves a woman who does not give evidence of self-restraint, harmless or otherwise.

HELPFUL HINTS FOR CORRECTNESS

HELPFUL HINTS FOR CORRECTNESS

HOW TO SAY "NO"

No one likes to be refused a request whatever it may be, but, in reflection, the one refused sometimes gains in respect for the person refusing and considers himself fortunate to have escaped the aftermath of a sickened conscience.

A blunt refusal may avoid an argument but it may also cause an unnecessary breach of friendly relations. There are so many ways of saying "No," not making it less firm, yet removing the culprit sort of feeling it so often leaves, especially between boy and girl acquaintances. Unfortunately, the cultivated familiarity on the part of the average girl or woman with men nowadays, with no intention of rudeness or licentiousness, has taken down so many rungs of the ladder of old time chivalry. A man often feels that the girl expects the customary thing, that he will lose out if he isn't aggressive.

Many boys have told me that a girl's refusal at first to be petted or kissed does not check his persistence, because it so often means that she admires his persistence, and wants to feel that she has been "wooed and won"; that the average girl feels that she has utterly failed of an evening's effort unless the young man with whom she spent it is not lured into holding her hands and offering to kiss her.

Poor clinging vines, spineless and often beautiful sirens! Can you, if you are sincere, find some way to have your boy friends feel that you do not expect to be kissed after the first date? Can you not get out of it without being rude? Why lead a really nice boy up to the door step, receiving his hand squeeze, coquetting with smiles and dancing eyes to lead him on, then cruelly and bluntly say, "I wouldn't think of doing that, what do you think I am?" Think it over beforehand. Don't bargain so readily for something you are not ready to accept. If you cuddle up on his shoulder in the car, if you pull on his arm on the way home from the movie, if your steps grow slower as you reach your front door, the dumbest man considers that an invitation to display sex interest and if he's enterprising in this modern age,, he'll dare anything.

Keep your conversation above sex; let it be impersonal. Talk about the picture, his pals, how proud you are of his football record, his place on the honor roll. Try to find something to swell his ego, and if he's really a gentleman you can feel safe with him. He'll forget that bewitching smile and indulge in a little self-glorification.

If he persists, just say, "You are making me so uncomfortable when I've been so happy with you," as pleasantly as possible, and that boy, if there is anything in him, will begin building up air castles of the home where he will take you some bright morning where, like the fairies, you will live happily ever-after.

One can say "No" pleasantly and mean it. Try it!

SHOPPING

1. Do not handle excessively merchandise which soils easily. Always remove gloves under such conditions.

2. Do not have a clerk bring out a great many dresses, shoes, coats, etc., when you know that you have no intention of purchasing anything.

3. Do not *order* a clerk to show you something. Always request, and don't forget to say "Please" and "I thank you."

4. If you remove something from a counter or rack to examine it, always return it to its place. If the clerk removes it, she will see that it is returned.

5. If you are going to buy shoes, be careful to see that your stockings are free of runs and holes in the feet. It is a good policy also to make this your first purchase. Then your feet will not have had so much chance to perspire from exercise.

6. Do not go to buy a hat when your hair has been freshly oiled. The clerk cannot risk having several hats soiled with grease.

7. When buying dresses, etc., be sure that your under-garments are fresh and in good condition and that you have taken particular care with your toilet. You owe it to yourself as well as to the clerk.

8. Do not stop in the aisles to carry on a conversation. If you must talk, step aside out of the other person's way.

9. Do not handle wearing apparel while smoking.

LET'S HAVE A GOOD TIME

Young people in these days are always looking for thrills—thrills and more thrills. They have literally run out of new ways of doing things, and the party becomes a bore unless there is crazy music, heel kicking, cocktails, dancing and more dancing to seductive music that makes everybody sleepy eyed and anxious to go to the porch or flower garden and sit out the rest of the evening on a bench.

What shall we do about it? I've lived ten miles from town and four miles from a railroad station for nearly forty years, with a group of all ages, all sizes, all temperaments, the grouch, the sophisticated, the innocent, the wise, the friendly, the shy.

Good times—you ask the kids. When school closes there are tears by the "buckets full." The happy home-going has vanished into "No more good times until fall." Well, how can we do it. It's a full-time job, but its success is the joy of our lives and we have had a good time doing it.

Perhaps the family will not find as much in this because we are a private boarding school, but I've known college classes to turn the time backward to grammar-school days in their glee and openly declare that they have had the time of their young lives.

The hikes, ending with a weiner roast on the edge of the woods as the sun begins to sink behind the western hills are never-forgotten experiences.

*For the House Party**

White elephant party	Magic writing
Kumsey Kum	Ghosts
The magic carpet	Simon says
Birds fly	Progressive games
Jenkins up	Menagerie.

Also

Molasses candy pull
Toasting marshmallows.

HINTS FOR THE GRADUATE

1. Never wear flowers with cap and gown.
2. See that the cap is straight on the head or just slightly tilted.
3. Sensible plain kid or dull patent pumps and hose usually uniform by class selection (no longer must it be gun metal or taupe) are in good taste.

* The author will be very glad to send written directions for any of the games here listed.

4. The tassel remains on the right for high school graduates. For college graduates the tassel is always turned to the left after receiving the degree.
5. Gifts for graduation should be immediately acknowledged.

CALLING

Calls, except those made by older, leisurely people, are almost passé. But certain obligations can be properly fulfilled only by this form of social intercourse.

FOR INSTANCE

1. It is expected that one call after a luncheon or dinner.
2. One should always acknowledge the announcement of a visitor for a few days by dropping in at least to meet the stranger or give a warm hand of welcome to someone met before.
3. The bride and groom who come to their new home are due a little visit at least from those who attended the wedding.
4. Calling on the sick or infirm to give a word of cheer or, even just to leave a card if the sick person cannot be seen, makes one feel that he is not forgotten.
5. Making people in your neighborhood feel comfortable with a call, whether or not they are one's social equals, is a gracious thing and has its own reward in the satisfaction usually sought by people who embrace Christianity as a source of ethics. This call may be supplemented by an invitation to visit "our Sunday School," or to hear "our minister" or to come to the lectures at "our Community Center."

It is a fine thing for younger men and younger women to make it their business to call occasionally for a chat with the friends of their parents, older people in the community.

I have in mind a splendid young college fellow, the son of friends in a nearby city, who always drives down for a little chat, however short the vacation. It is one of the anticipated joys of the season to look forward to David's visit and hear all about the college boys and girls, the games and stunts of college life—house parties, week-ends, etc.

A revival of the "old time hitching Dobbin to the Sled" and taking the whole family to spend an evening popping corn, toasting marshmallows and playing games, ending with the delicious repast of cider and doughnuts, would remake America.

DOORS

Did it ever occur to you, young friend, that your fortune or misfortune lies behind the door you are about to open? Then be careful how you open it. Slamming and banging doors are childish traits not overcome by older boys and girls, and mark one as poorly bred. Many an applicant for a job has lost his chance because he abruptly opened the door of his employer and failed to close it as he went out from the interview.

If one must knock on the door of a room or office, it must be a gentle tapping. When bidden to enter, take firm hold on the knob, turn it gently, pull the door open at least two-thirds of the way so as not to touch either the door or door jamb, pause for just a second to recognize the person who may be looking your way, and as gently close the door as you opened it. Do not make the mistake of letting a self-closing door push you into the room, for it will embarrass you and prevent you from presenting your best appearance. Your doom may be sealed before you speak a word.

If you must go through several doors that require opening before reaching the main one, be sure that each is quietly closed behind you.

A house is often said to be a man's castle. One should not enter without invitation. So it is with the individual's room, whatever the relation. An understanding that you are not intruding upon one's privacy is the only excuse for entering a door already open. One should always knock on a closed door, except when personally attending to one in a sick room.

In buildings where the offices are not particularly private one does not knock. It is the custom to enter. If the conversation or business going on seems in the least private, one withdraws to the outside unless the person in charge recognizes the newcomer and bids him stay. If one is uncertain and his business is of such importance as to make a special appointment, it is never considered rude to interrupt by using the nearest telephone and making an appointment.

A gentleman opens a door and permits a lady to precede him, going in or out. A young woman offers the same courtesy to an older woman.

If someone is following you immediately out of a door, a man following a man or a woman of seemingly equal status or age following a man or woman, it is not necessary to stand and hold the door ajar unless it is self-closing, but see that it is left open. It would be wise to pause and see if the door was closed properly. If not, your knowledge of good breeding would cover up that breach.

In theatres or public places where doormen open and close doors for you alone and those accompanying you, a nod of the head in appreciation is a sign of good breeding.

BUSINESS ETIQUETTE

Politeness costs nothing but goes farther than money in making friends and establishing one's place in society.

Subordinates in office, secretaries, office boys, etc., should rise when their employers enter the office for the first time in the day, and unless bidden to remain seated, should rise for the discussion of any matter broached by the employer.

"Yes, Mr. A." and "No, Mr. B." is the proper form for one- or two-word answers. A nod of the head or a "Yes" or "No" in courteous tones should follow succeeding questions requiring one-word answers. "Yes, Sir" and "Yes, Madam," are outmoded except for house servants by people generally, but they are always in good taste for one's elders or superiors in office.

Men do not generally remove their hats in elevators now, especially in office buildings, but the thoughtful man continues to remove his hat in the presence of ladies in a room, even though it is as small as the elevator.

Don't argue with the employer. Assume at least that he is right.

Answer promptly always. Don't be afraid of being too courteous.

Go out of your way to serve your employer. He will remember the little kindnesses not included in the pay envelope in a larger way some day.

TELEGRAMS

Sometime ago telegrams were used only in extreme cases but now they have become a part of common correspondence so much so that the companies operating for that purpose make all kinds of inducements numbered to suit the varying mood of individuals at such reduced rates that the popular favor substitute them for greeting cards, small gifts and remembrances.

For business purposes, however, young people need to differentiate between day letters, straight telegrams, and night letters because the prices vary according to the type.

A straight message, usually ten words, for a stated price must be succinct, but must convey the message or a request. For an instance:

STRAIGHT TELEGRAM

April 15, 1940

North Carolina Mutual Life Insurance Co.
Durham, North Carolina
Wiring premium, Industrial Policy B, 1007.

B. J. W. Grier

TOURATE—SPECIAL RATE

Madam Sara Spencer Washington
Apex News and Hair Company
Atlantic City, New Jersey
Joan arriving Thirtieth Street Station, 9:45 Tuesday evening.

Althea M. Jones
House Director

NIGHT LETTER

(25 words same as day letter, reduced rates for extra words)
The Brices
400 Manhattan Avenue, Apt. 71
New York City
We note with pride Jonathan's part in the play, "John Henry," staged on Broadway last night. Critics praise of music interesting. Sorry story did not take. Better luck next time.

Eugene A. Brice

DAY LETTER

(First 10 words regular rate. Up to fifty words cheaper
than straight telegram.)

Miss Mae Belcher
653 North West Street
Indianapolis, Indiana

Regret exceedingly my inability to be present at the anniversary celebration of your services in connection with
the Y.W.C.A. Dr. Mary McLeod Bethune will bring my
greetings, and I have asked Mrs. John Hope to say something of our Y Hut project. Continued good wishes for the
success of your splendid institution.

Marian B. Wilkinson

CABLEGRAM

(Most expensive medium of communication between countries. Sometimes costs as high as one or two dollars per word. Usually used to
acquaint relatives or businesses of safe arrival. Business people have
established codes.)

Mrs. F. D. Patterson
Tuskegee, Alabama

London on date scheduled.

R. R. Moton

RADIOGRAM

(Equally expensive as above)

W. G. Pearson
Queen Mary
Enroute, Mid-Ocean

Shepard, Spaulding, Kennedy, Merrick awaiting London
Dock.

J. W. Seabrook

(This would mean that these men were at the London
dock to greet W. G. Pearson.)

VISITING CARDS

If one wishes an address on the visiting card, it should be written in the right-hand corner.

MISS CHARLOTTE EUGENIA HAWKINS
69 Dana Street
Cambridge, Massachusetts

If the visiting card is large it may be used for invitations or short messages.

Leave cards after a formal call for the hostess and guests or guest of honor, one for each guest.

For invitation, write on the card:

MRS. WILLIAM STUART NELSON
Tuesday, January 11
Tea at 5 o'clock

A visiting card may be used to reply to an invitation (written on the face).

Glad to accept your kind invitation for Friday, at 2 o'clock; or—

Regret cannot be present at Tea on Friday at 2 o'clock.

Cards may express condolence written on the back.

Sorry for the sadness which was yours. Deepest sympathy.

Cards may be used to accompany gifts.

LETTER WRITING

Here, follow the rules of English. Be sure to make your letters a part of your personality and cheerful and interesting. Remember girls, don't write sentimental letters to boys and make it the law of your life never to write a letter that will make you ashamed if read in public.

Clergymen

Address: The Reverend John Brice or John Brice, D.D.
Salutation: Sir, My dear Sir, or Dear Dr. Brice.
Closing: Respectfully yours, or Yours Sincerely, Yours faithfully

Doctor

Address: Dr. T. Edward Jones, or T. Edward Jones, M.D.
Salutation: Sir, My dear Sir, or Dear Dr. Jones
Closing: Very truly yours, or Yours truly

Professor

Address: Professor Walter English or Walter English, Prof.
Salutation: Dear Professor English or Dear Dr. English
Closing: Yours faithfully, or Sincerely yours

MISCELLANEOUS

1. Should men help ladies out of cars? Should men leave street cars or busses before ladies?

   Ans. Men should always offer their hand to ladies when entering or alighting from cars or descending from steps. The man precedes the woman out of the car or bus, steps down first. The woman precedes going in, the man lifting her by the arm up the step.

2. Should a young man help a young lady up the stairs?

   Ans. Ordinarily no. In modern days, he is gracious beyond expectation when he does, except the steps are steep like in theatres.

3. Should a young man "tip" his hat to a lady who is not known to him?

   Ans. Under certain circumstances.

   a. Accidently bumps into her.
   b. Acknowledgment of a courtesy or favor.
   c. If a lady recognizes him first.

4. Should a gentleman escort a lady into her house after attending a party?

Ans. Ordinarily, no. If residence is in an apartment house with hallways, etc. he sees her to her own door.

5. When is it proper for a young lady to take a young man's arm?

Ans. When crossing the floor of a dance hall or when walking along at night for protection against stumbling.

6. Should a fourteen-year-old girl accept a gift from a boy? Should she give a boy a present?

Ans. Not without consent of parents or guardians should she receive or give presents and the gift should be inexpensive.

7. Should a man ever carry a young lady's hand bag as is sometimes seen?

Ans. According to the meaning of hand bag. If it means a heavy hand bag, clothes, etc., yes. If purse, coin, handkerchief, paper, no. He should not be burdened with small bags and packages.

8. Is it proper for a young lady to lend a young man money?

Ans. Only under exceptional circumstances. Real men avoid such a situation.

9. Should a gentleman offer to pay a young lady friend's fare if they should meet on street car or bus?

Ans. He need not feel compelled to do so. Not wholly improper but girls of good taste will refuse graciously. If the young man insists, she will accept rather than cause a scene.

10. Should a young man of no kin visit the bedroom of his girl friend who is ill?

Ans. Not without the presence of some one in authority or the nurse. In isolated cases, he may be in her presence alone but should leave the door open. It is permissible now for young men to visit young women in hospitals.

11. If parents have enough confidence in a boy to permit him to pay attention to their daughter, do you think the mother should open and read the girl's mail if she is old enough to have a sweetheart?

Ans. No. Parents should permit girls to open own mail but confidence and relationships should be such that daughter would want mother to enjoy her mail with her. Boys should have desire to write only such letters as could be read by mothers and understood even though it might carry a vein of love.

12. If a couple is visiting and it is time to leave, should the lady rise first?

Ans. Yes. It is the part of the lady to indicate their readiness to leave. If the young man thinks they should depart, he makes a sign to the young woman and she rises to make the first move.

13. Why do younger girls have a tendency to ignore elders?

Ans. It is merely a youthful tendency to be smart and to assume a certain degree of independence.

14. When can one chew gum in public?

Ans. It is permissible when engaging in some sport such as football, basketball, or tennis. Spectators at such events may chew gum also, provided it is not accompanied by loud "smacking, cracking or popping."

15. When may a girl take a man's arm?

Ans. When the road is hazardous or going through a crowd or when trying to keep up with him. There is this exception. Older women may lean upon the arm of their husband or young man in order that their steps may be steadied.

16. Shall the man let the lady precede him going upstairs?

Ans. The man precedes the lady upstairs and follows her down.

17. Is it ever correct for a girl to meet a man at a public place?

Ans. In these days when men and women both work it is permissible for young women to meet a young man in the lobby of the hotel or restaurant at a certain time. She should never hang around the door but should find a convenient place to sit or stand on the inside that she may see him when he appears. This meeting should only be done under unavoidable circumstances.

18. In entering a restaurant must the girl lead the way to a seat? Must she give the order?

Ans. If there is no one to take you to a seat, the young woman may choose the table at which she would like to sit, but the young man is supposed to give the order when he finds out what she wants.

19. Is it correct for a lady to hold a gentleman's coat for him to put it on?

Ans. A woman does not assist a man in and out of his coat unless he is old, feeble or an invalid.

20. What are the courtesies due a chaperone at a social function?

Ans. The term "chaperone" is obsolete. This term has been replaced by "hostess," and the hostess has a definite function. She may be approached for introductions, in emergencies, or over any question that may arise. She should never be neglected during the dance. If she enjoys dancing, several of the boys should courteously ask her to dance. If refreshments are served, it is imperative that the hostess be served among the first and that she eat with the others. The guests should never leave without expressing pleasure and appreciation for her kindness in making the party a success.

21. At a dinner party should the young man dance first with the hostess or with the young lady he escorted?

    Ans. He dances first with the young lady he escorted. He should invite his hostess and her guest of honor to dance with him at least once.

22. When one is at a party or tea and does not desire to participate in the games, what should one do?

    Ans. Such a person should remain at home. But if he is present, he should make himself agreeable with anything that is prepared for his entertainment. Every person, however, who plans to go into society of any sort should learn to dance and play cards.

23. When taken out by a gentleman, should the girl tell him where she wishes to go?

    Ans. If the young man asks her where she would like to go, she may state her preference. Otherwise, she accepts the plans of her host when she accepts his invitation.

24. Where must a man walk when accompanying two ladies?

    Ans. Next to the curb. Never between two ladies.

25. When on the train or in a restaurant, where food is served in little dishes, should it be eaten from them or transferred to the main plate?

    Ans. It is better to eat the food from the small dishes in which it is placed.

26. How must young girls have their calling cards made?

    Ans. Size 2¾ x 2. They should be engraved. The Miss or Mrs. should precede the whole name. The address, if any, should be in the right hand corner.

27. What must one do who wishes to speak to a very busy person, of business or of necessity?

    Ans. Watch the speaker, and at a pause say, "Excuse me please, but may I speak to you for a moment?"

28. How long after a visit must a bread-and-butter letter be written?

    Ans. Certainly within one week.

29. What does R.S.V.P. mean?

    Ans.   Répondez s'il vous plaît, means answer if you please.   It should be regarded as a sacred request with which to comply as soon as possible.

30. When you are at home and answering the telephone, is it correct to say "Hello?"

    Ans.   See chapter 17 on the correct way to answer the telephone.

31. When you have succeeded in securing your number when making a telephone call, is it correct to ask who is speaking?

    Ans.   See chapter 17 on the correct way to answer the telephone.

32. Should a man who has been working all day and is sitting in a street car give his seat to a lady who is standing?

    Ans.   He should at least offer the courtesy.

33. Should a young person give in to an older person in a discussion to avoid prolonged argument when the younger person has definite proof of the elder's error?

    Ans.   It would be the polite thing to do to stop the discussion.   One need not give in.

34. How should a boy open an inward-swing door for a girl?

    Ans.   Take hold of the knob, place his hand on the outside and hold it until she passes through.

35. Should a week-end guest leave the hostess a gift or send it?

    Ans.   Either may be correct.

36. Should young ladies smoke to be sociable?

    Ans.   Not unless they are in the habit of smoking.   (See chapter on smoking.)

37. What is the proper use of cosmetics for school?

    Ans.   Just as little as possible to appear natural looking is best for students.

38. Should the glove be removed when offering the hand on the street?

    Ans.   A lady never does, but a gentleman does.

39. Is it permissible for a young girl to entertain in her house coat in the morning?

    Ans.   She should never entertain a gentleman in her house coat. It is permissible, however, for her to entertain girl friends or women who may be her house guest or unexpected guests.

40. How can one break an awkward silence in a group?

    Ans.   By making mention of anything in which people are generally interested; weather, movie, books, etc.

41. Must guests stop to say goodnight to their hostess before leaving?
    Ans. Yes, guests should stop by and say goodnight to the hostess before leaving.

42. When riding with a man in a taxicab, must he announce the street and number?
    Ans. Yes.

43. Are there times when a young man's coat should be buttoned, especially the double breasted style?
    Ans. It is good form to button the lower button of a double breasted coat. Now-a-days when men wear the short coats to sport dances, etc., they should never be left to hang open.

44. If a girl is sitting conversing with her escort, is it proper for her to accept a dance with another young man? If so, what should the girl say to her escort?
    Ans. Yes. She should excuse herself and accept the dance.

BIBLIOGRAPHY

This book has been almost wholly written out of the ideals, observations and practices growing out of the experiences of the Palmer Memorial Institute as from time to time we have sought information by visits, reading, conversations, suggestions of faculty and interested friends. No attempt has been made to copy either the form or content of any one book or number of books. Knowing that we could not wholly establish a code of etiquette of our own, we have checked our practices by those recognized authorities in etiquette and social culture, and here list a bibliography for those who desire to go more deeply into the subjects here briefly discussed.

Personality: Prentice-Hall, Inc.
Etiquette: Emily Post
Charm: Margery Wilson
Gentlemen Behave: Charles H. Townes
Good Manners: Bertha Bailey McLean
Everyday Manners: Ruth Wanger, and others
Manners for Millions: Hadida
English in Action: Tressler
Girl Today; Woman Tomorrow: Hunter
Standard Etiquette: Anna S. Richards
Social Usage Leaflets: Teacher's College, Columbia University.

Most of the questions are those that have been asked by students and faculty members in preparation for the personal culture classes given in this institution as part of the regular course of study.

ABOUT THE EDITORS

Henry Louis Gates, Jr., is the W. E. B. Du Bois Professor of the Humanities, Chair of the Afro-American Studies Department, and Director of the W. E. B. Du Bois Institute for Afro-American Research at Harvard University. One of the leading scholars of African-American literature and culture, he is the author of *Figures in Black: Words, Signs, and the Racial Self* (1987), *The Signifying Monkey: A Theory of Afro-American Literary Criticism* (1988), *Loose Canons: Notes on the Culture Wars* (1992), and the memoir *Colored People* (1994).

Jennifer Burton is in the Ph.D. program in English Language and Literature at Harvard University. She is the volume editor of *The Prize Plays and Other One-Acts* in this series. She was a contributor to *Great Lives from History: American Women*, and, with her mother and sister, coauthored two one-act plays, *Rita's Haircut* and *Litany of the Clothes*. Her creative non-fiction has appeared in *There and Back* and *Buffalo*, the Sunday magazine of the *Buffalo News*.

Carolyn C. Denard is Associate Professor of English at Georgia State University. Her published works focus on twentieth-century African-American literature and cultural history. She is currently completing a book manuscript on the uses of memory in the works of contemporary African-American writers who grew up in the Jim Crow South and a book on the uses of myth and history in the fiction of Toni Morrison.

Gramley Library
Salem College
Winston-Salem, NC 27108